GROWING STUDENTS BY
EMPOWERING TEACHERS

BOLD
HUMILITY

DR. DAVID M. SCHMITTOU

A very special "Thank you" to my oldest son, Cameron, who was able to come up with such amazing cover art. At 13 years old, you truly amaze me. Thank you for visually capturing so much: Leadership comes full circle from boldness to humility. It is not a smooth line, nor is it an easy circle to complete, but you captured the essence.
You, Cameron, have a gift!

Bold Humility: Growing Students by Empowering Teachers

Copyright © 2019 by David M. Schmittou

Published by EduGladiators LLC

www.edugladiators.com

Book Design & Production: EduGladiators LLC

Paperback ISBN: 978-1-7336864-8-8

ebook ISBN: 978-1-7336864-9-5

CONTENTS

FOREWORD   ix

INTRODUCTION   xi

CHAPTER ONE   1

CHAPTER TWO   14

CHAPTER THREE   29

CHAPTER FOUR   46

CHAPTER FIVE   60

CHAPTER SIX   78

CHAPTER SEVEN   94

CHAPTER EIGHT   110

CHAPTER NINE   122

CHAPTER TEN   132

MORE FROM EDUGLADIATORS   134

FOREWORD
BY BRIAN MENDLER

Author, speaker, teacher, friend, Twitter @BrianMendler

Relationships. It's all about relationships. We say relationships are needed to help teach our students content, but the reality is, the content we teach our students, we teach them so that in life they can have productive relationships. It's not the other way around, or at least it shouldn't be. The truth is, this is not just wisdom that applies to students. It is also relevant to the adults who work in schools.

I first met Dave several years ago when I was presenting a workshop on helping "That One Kid". I was sharing ideas and concepts on how to engage with kids that we often push aside and how to use what is often their greatest strength, their confidence, and swagger, to our advantage. At the end of the workshop, Dave came up, asked me to sign a copy of a book he bought, then took a selfie with me. That selfie allowed us to form a friendship that has allowed each of us to grow professionally and personally.

When Dave posted the selfie on-line, comments started flooding in from our common friends commenting on the similarities between the two of us. People have told us that we look like brothers. We are both follically challenged (bald just sounds too critical). We are both about the same age. We both get to speak to schools and audiences around the country. In the years since then, he and I have learned more, not only about our similarities, but also about the differences we possess, differences that allow each of us to grow.

Dave has helped share with some of the groups I have presented to. I have likewise consulted him and his staff on effective classroom management strategies and processes. We share with each other on social media, through text, and on the phone. We understand and appreciate each other. We lean on each other for support, for confidence, and for opportunities to grow. That's what Bold Humility is all about.

In this book, Dave describes for us all how to use our existing relationships, and those we are yet to form, to grow who we are individually and collectively. He reminds us all that we have to be bold enough to celebrate our strengths and what makes us unique while also embracing our struggles, with humility, by learning to lean on others.

Relationships are not a means to an end. They are the end. In schools, we have to teach content. We have to teach subject matter, and we have to remember, our job is not just to make good students, but good people.

Kids become what they see. I hope that you will dive into this book and begin to reflect on what you do, why you do it, and how you can do it better, because kids are always watching. If it is about That One Kid, we also have to remember That One Kid deserves each of us doing our part to grow, to improve, to be Bold, to show Humility, and to embrace the why behind the what. If you are a leader, by title or by default, your followers, whether they are kids or adults will be what you are. I hope you will take the lessons in these pages and apply them because That One Kid, all of those kids, That One Teacher, all of those teachers, deserve it.

INTRODUCTION

Who You Are is Who They Will Be

Compassionate. Honest. Focused. Cheerful. Curious. Diplomatic. Flexible. Bold. Humble.

It would be amazing to have the people I work with describe me with any of the words listed above. I have had the opportunity to fill a lot of roles in public education from classroom teacher to a central office administrator, but my favorite by far was serving as a school principal. As a public school principal, I was blessed to work with some amazing people. People who chose their career not because of the paychecks they received, or the fame and notoriety they would get from society. I got to work with people who served a purpose so much larger than their own. I worked with people who receive wages that simply allow them to keep living their purpose. I worked with people who believe they have a calling and the work they do is a service.

As a school principal my primary responsibility was to hire the people I wished to place in front of the next generation of the workforce. As I hired teachers, support staff, custodians, cafeteria workers, and secretaries, I used the same criteria every single time. I did not look at certifications, education, and work experience beyond minimum qualifications as defined by the human resources department of my district. I looked for people who focused on being quality people. A high achieving professional is a byproduct of being a high-quality person. It does not always work the other way around.

As a school administrator, I know my job is to help create future successful adults. I do this by placing successful adults in front of the children in my charge. Kids will become what they see. Trends and fads do not become popular among kids and teenagers because somebody stands in front of them telling them how to dress, how to talk, or how to act. Kids mimic what they see others doing. As kids work their way through adolescence they will begin to wrestle with what it means to be an adult. Their definition of success will emerge from examining the adults in their lives, the adults they encounter at home, at church, at the mall, and at school. If we want to create kids who become high quality people, we must be adults of high quality.

Influence has nothing to do with a placard or a title. I know this because at home I am known as "dad" and quite often I am simply at the whim of everyone else in the household. My title carries with it very little influence. Being outnumbered by my four kids, I know that a mutiny can happen at any time. At work, I have been a teacher, coach, principal, and director. I am an evaluator. I am an administrator. I have dozens of workplace tasks that define my role, but none of them define my power and influence. 2500 kids, 150 staff members, only 1 me. My title may give me some authority, but authority without influence, matters little.

Too often in organizations, we see individuals who carry with them the title "boss" and erroneously believe that this also equates to influence. Often it is the "boss" who makes the biggest miscalculation. I absolutely believe that respect is given and not earned. I wholeheartedly believe that respect is a basic human right. That is not to say that respect, authority, and power all equate to influence. Influence and the power to change thoughts, actions, and beliefs very rarely come from positional authority.

I have had the opportunity to work in a number of schools in multiple states. I get the chance to speak with educators across the country discussing the ideas behind this book and the last book I wrote, *It's Like Riding a Bike: How to Make Learning Last a Lifetime* (shameless plug), and have encountered so many others who share my belief, that we are in the life changing business. There are some amazing teachers and administrators across this country who are still in touch with the reason they got into this profession. But unfortunately, that truth is not universal. There are some who have been set adrift. There are some who have been corrupted by the media, the state and federal legislation that has attempted to distill individual children into collective quantitative data, and even the other negative voices in their buildings and across the hall. Sometimes it feels as though everyone working in schools has lost their purpose so it is just easier to give up the fight and join the ranks of the negative, the ranks of the lost, the ranks who resemble a boat adrift in a storm as opposed to believing the ship has a captain passing out life jackets while he himself grabs the oars and begins to push through the waves keeping those in his charge feeling safe and optimistic knowing that every storm is temporary.

The purpose of this book is to remind you all that good captains do exist. If you are one of those educators who have been set adrift, let this book serve as your anchor. Let it stop you from moving any further. Let it keep you grounded so that once the storms pass you can begin to move towards the horizon again. If you are an educator who still believes you can focus on each child as opposed to every child yes- there is a difference- this book is for you. I hope that we can all use this book as a reflective lens to examine our own practices knowing that others are always watching and what they see, they will do. I challenge you to have the confidence to stay true to your principles, to be bold enough to fight the fights that need fighting, yet willing to explore your own practices and beliefs to realize that you may not have everything figured out.

Humility is a result of vulnerability and a willingness to grow and improve. Boldness implies the confidence to pursue excellence and to embrace your gifts. Bold Humility is the secret sauce of destiny changers. It is the "it factor" I look for in hiring others to join my team. It is what separates the quality professional from the quality person, and I hope this book helps you understand the difference. My job as a leader has three major components: hire the best, challenge the best, and cheer for the best. Although I may not have had a direct hand on your appointment in your current school, I hope this book allows you to feel recruited to the profession again, to feel valued, and to feel inspired to grow a little bit more each day. I hope that as you read through these pages you begin to feel more like those opening words to this book, "Compassionate. Honest. Focused. Cheerful. Curious. Diplomatic. Flexible. Bold. Humble" than you have in a long time and that as a result, your influence and example can help foster the same beliefs in the students you impact.

I have heard many administrators make the statement "I do everything for the kids." This is an amazing mindset and one that I hold on to. This does not mean that in working with and for your students that you make the lives of the adults miserable. If you want to enhance the lives of your students, work to enhance the lives of those on the front lines. Only once a leader realizes his or her ability to lead depends more on those who follow, and his or her ability to serve them, will change begin taking root.

If you really want to see where the power and influence exists in any organization, get a hold of the salary scale, turn it upside down, then start with the top. Real leaders understand that **Bold Humility** is what gets the job done.

 "Principals: If it's all about the kids, make it about the teachers. When they are growing so are your kids."

CHAPTER ONE

My Story

I AM A DISASTER. I am not an expert at anything except making mistakes, but at least I know that. I have learned so much throughout my career, but perhaps the single greatest lesson I have learned is how to recover from my imperfections. This book will not be a "how to" guide, but may actually at times serve as a "how NOT to" guide. My hope is that through this reflective manifesto you will not only learn from my successes, but my failures as well. Yes, I will be providing examples and lessons of some things that have gone right and yes, I hope to inspire you to be the teacher and the leader your staff and students need and deserve, but I am not perfect, not by a long shot. I am flawed. I have made countless mistakes and I am nowhere close to having all of the answers to the questions I face in any of the roles I possess, but I also believe this is part of what adds credibility to what you will be reading. Sometimes the willingness to admit your weaknesses is actually your greatest strength.

I believe leaders should work to become KNOWable more than KNOWLEDGEable. I believe that we follow people, not positions. So, who am I? What makes me tick? What are my priorities?

I am a father. I have four amazing kids. At the time this is being written, my oldest child is in middle school and my youngest is about to begin pre-k. I am a busy man, but I smile often, primarily because my kids are amazing. They are the reason I do what I do, why I work hard, and they are the reason I try to get better every day. I am working on improving and growing because I am BROKEN. Wow, am I ever?! I have been on this earth for 41 years and have spent 40 of them trying to convince everyone that I make no mistakes. I have wanted everyone to think I am the smartest, funniest, most charismatic person around. I post on social media all kinds of great clips highlighting my success. I used to think one of my responsibilities in life was to be my own personal publicists, but the only person I was fooling was myself. Everyone already saw through it. People already saw all of the mistakes I made. They saw me trying to cover up my insecurities. Instead of seeing me as a man who was humble and willing to own his shortcomings, many saw me as arrogant and unwavering. It wasn't until recently that I realized how flawed everyone already perceived me to be that I fully embraced my willingness to grow.

You see, for my entire life I compared myself to other people. I always wanted to be the best person around. Best is a relative term. If I knew someone else was better than I was at anything, I simply avoided that person. If I felt I was getting close enough for someone to recognize my struggles, I pushed them away with a stiff arm. If I saw that I had strengths that were relatively stronger than others, I would jump all in to show them off causing others to reject me. I spent the better part of my life feeling alone, not because others were not around me, but because I worked actively to live in an invented bubble.

In 2018 I entered counseling as a result of these realizations. Soon after that I also started taking medication to help with some of these internal struggles. I am now at a place where I am not comparing myself to others. I am working on me. I am working to become a better version of me, a version of me who owns his strengths and works on his struggles, a me who is willing to be vulnerable as well as confident, a me who is strong enough to just be me. I am sharing all of this for several reasons.

1. As a professional educator, I recognize the need to raise the next generation to compete globally, but I also recognize that we only compete globally when we create a generation of passion seekers. We must work to create kids who are comfortable in their own skin, kids who know who they are, and are willing to embrace their passions to change the world. We cannot foster a system that makes kids ever feel "less than" as this simply fosters the society we have now, a society unwilling to accept feedback and a society unwilling to grow and change. A society that gravitates towards the safety of the masses as opposed to the original. If your school, classroom, or household has policies and practices that compares, sorts, selects, identifies, and labels, please start the conversation on how you can begin to celebrate, embrace, and endorse instead. Kids do not need us adding to their pressure to conform. They need us to celebrate who they are.

2. How we treat our kids impacts the adults they become, but...focusing on who they can become distracts from who they are. Kids are not simply preparing for their life, they are in the midst of living their life. Just as a 41 year old adult, I am working to improve who I am, so are 5 year olds, 12 year olds, and 25 year olds....as are 70 year olds, and 90 year olds. We must embrace who we are TODAY to improve who we will be tomorrow. If you are a teacher, make experiences relevant for your students today. Let them embrace being a kid. When we force kids to focus on the future, the distant future, they begin to chase rainbows instead of picking the daisies. Try to never start a sentence with "I can't wait until..." and embrace the moment. When you chase the next best thing or encourage others to do so, you are already comparing where you are to where others have arrived.

3. I know vulnerability is critical for establishing trust. If you are like me and feel the need to compete with others, stop. Embrace you. People will be more receptive to what you have to say

when they know that what you have to say is genuine. A genuine person knows what they know and admits what they don't. Bold Humility is the secret sauce to success.

4. If you are a teacher, your kids already see your weaknesses. If you are a leader, your followers already know your flaws. As a politician once said, "You can't put lipstick on a pig." When you try to hide mistakes, you deny your ability to grow and you make it that much more difficult for others to learn from you. When people see you as a fraud and fake, no matter how profound your thoughts, your wisdom is already dismissed. The best teachers and leaders are often the most genuine.

We will cover each of these concepts in greater detail later in this book, but I feel it is extremely important for me to share more about me, as a person and a professional to help you gain a little more context at this time. My strengths and my struggles define me. It is critical that I am open and honest about where I have been, where I am going, and who I am today. It is this person who is trying to inspire change and growth for so many others, but it starts with me.

Where it All Began

Professionally, I began my career in education nineteen years ago. I graduated with my Bachelors' degree in December of 1999, did some substitute teaching for a semester and then began interviewing for my first teaching job. Back then, seemingly everyone was being steered towards a career in education. Finding a teaching job was an extremely competitive endeavor, but I was lucky enough to receive job offers to be a full-time middle school teacher from two districts.

One of the schools that offered me a job was the comfortable surroundings where I had been a student teacher. While student teaching, I served as a coach for multiple sports, was an after-school tutor, and built a lot of amazing relationships.

The other school that offered me a job was in a large district where I would be one of 100 new teachers being hired. I knew nobody and had never stepped foot inside any of the classrooms. It was an affluent district with a great reputation, but I had no personal connection to it.

It should have been an easy decision for me, but deciding where to begin my career was difficult. There were a lot of variables to consider and wrestle with, but ultimately, I made the decision to explore the new school and to move on from the place that opened its doors to me as a student teacher and to begin working in a school district that was new, wealthy, and exciting.

Some of my friends and family believed I made the decision to pursue a school that presented more opportunities and a more affluent student population. Some thought I wanted a new challenge. But the truth of the matter was, that as a 22 year old, right out of college, only one thing really mattered to me. I accepted the annual contract that paid $500 more. I remember my starting salary to this day: $34,734. I did not look at long-range salary implications, professional growth opportunities, stability, or relational capacity. At that point in my life, I was willing to dismiss relationships, stability, and comfort for $500. In college, I didn't decide to pursue education as a career because of the financial gain, but that was the deciding factor I used when deciding where to begin my career. It embarrasses me to this day that such a relatively small amount of money influenced my decision, but the reality is, it did. And the truth of the matter is, financial gain has actually impacted my decision to accept other jobs as well. This isn't necessarily a bad thing, but, beginning my career by sacrificing things that were important to me, people and comfort, for $500 probably wasn't the best way to begin making adult decisions and establishing adult habits.

During my first year of full-time teaching, I quickly realized that the students I was teaching were not like the students I had taught the previous year. These students came with background knowledge. Their parents had resources and as a result, in my head, teaching was so much easier. I was rocking this teaching thing. Why did everyone say that my first year would be so difficult? I kept telling myself I had everything figured out. By Christmas of year one, I was already coming to the conclusion that I should leave the classroom and begin working as a school administrator. I just knew that I was so good, I should be telling everyone else how to teach like me. I was a cocky rookie teacher and that arrogant attitude did not win me a lot of teacher friends early on.

It took me the next eighteen months to complete my Masters' program and to earn my credentials to be a school administrator. Two years into my teaching career and I believed I now had everything needed to lead others. I thought I knew everything about being a great teacher because I was one. I now even had a Masters' degree in Educational Leadership proving that I was a leader in all things education. All I needed now was for the right job opportunity to open up. I knew I probably wouldn't be able to get a full principalship yet, but surely, I wouldn't have a problem becoming an assistant principal. Who wouldn't want to hire such an amazing educator?

The summer in between my second and third years of teaching, armed with a new Masters' degree in my hand and all of the unwarranted confidence I could muster, I went on 16 job interviews. **SIXTEEN**. And yes, I did say there was a third year of teaching that was to come. This, not too subtle, foreshadowing demonstrates that I did not become a school administrator at that point. As a matter of fact, I didn't get a single offer. I interviewed at elementary schools, middle schools, high schools, charter schools, public schools, and private schools. I did get two callbacks from superintendents during that summer, however, neither had any desire to hire me, but each in his own way wanted to sit me down and let me know that I was way too young, lacked any real experience, and really didn't know what I was getting myself into. They wanted to give me feedback they knew I needed to hear, even if I wasn't ready to listen to it.

Jumping into my third year as a teacher, I was bitter. I did not listen to the wisdom being shared with me. The nonverbal feedback presented by not getting job offers was not welcomed. I rejected it just like I was rejected, and I was mad. In my mind, every school in the state of Michigan, where I was interviewing, was missing out on greatness. They didn't know how good I was and what I could deliver. As a result, I made yet another poor decision. I decided maybe teaching wasn't going to be my career. Maybe I needed "more" and deserved "more. I began to think that maybe I was too smart for the broken-down system that I saw as public education and if I couldn't get the opportunity to fix it from the inside I would do so from the outside. I decided to begin attending law school at nights. I made the decision that I would become a lawyer who would serve as an advocate for parents who also saw the same incompetence from schools that I did and needed a voice from the inside to help them gain clarity and the change they sought. I decided I would continue to teach during the day while attending law school in the evenings. It was an ambitious plan, but one that I thought I could manage and succeed at. And I did, for exactly one year.

In June of 2003, after attending law school for a year, and finishing up my third year as a teacher, I was contacted by the Director of Human Resources for my school district who asked me to meet with him the following day. That meeting was perhaps the single most impactful conversation I have ever had as a professional. I remember walking into the director's large office and being told to sit down. Seated across from this man, who was thirty years my senior, I felt nervous for the first time in a long time and that feeling did not ease up. I did not know why I was so anxious, but I remember feeling intimidated and scared.

For the next fifteen minutes I was told how hard GOOD teaching was. I was told that if I thought my job was EASY then I was obviously not as good as I thought. In this large district, a district of more than 5,000 teachers, the director knew who I was and knew that I had gone on a number of interviews the year before. I was earning a reputation, but it wasn't for being an up and coming superstar. He knew I was in law school seeking a potential career change and he wanted to give me some advice. His advice was simple, yet profound, as it forever changed the course of my career. Looking me directly in the eyes he stated, "Quit chasing the next best thing. It's like looking for the end of the rainbow. You will never find it. Just embrace where you are. Go all in and when you do you will achieve greatness. Once you have achieved greatness by chasing your passion, doors will open. You will never be able to kick down a door that was not meant for you to open." I promise you, this is an exact quote. Time literally stood still as this conversation played out. For the first time in a long time, I was humbled. He was so right. I was so sure that I deserved a promotion that I lost sight of where I was and I had to be honest, I wasn't working hard and my students were not getting my best.

We finished that meeting with an understanding and a change in direction. I was being transferred to another middle school in the district to teach and to get a fresh start. From that fresh start, I have had a passion that has been burning for sixteen years with no sign of going out, and I no longer begin my sentences with, "I can't wait until..." I embrace where I am, when I am there, and go all in.

In my new building I coached four sports, I won Teacher of the Year as voted on by students and found myself exhausted each night after pouring my heart and soul into being the best teacher I could be. I felt the change and my students and peers noticed a difference, so much so, that at the end of my eighth year, after not going on any interviews for the previous five years, the school district decided to create a new administrative position for me. A new Director of Human Resources was in place at this time. He called me up one afternoon to explain that my reputation, a new reputation of being a dedicated and hardworking teacher, had earned me a new opportunity, an opportunity that I did not seek out, but one that I was made to fill. I graciously and eagerly accepted the position and my administrative career officially began.

In that newly created position (we called it a Dean of Students position) I was able to meet with students, to cultivate relationships with parents, to lead the district's Talented and Gifted program, and to work with small groups of at-risk students. It was a catch-all position that taught me so much and allowed me to stroke my passion flames a little higher. I felt alive and fully embraced where I was. Then, just a year into serving in this position, I was contacted, out of the blue, by another school district nearby. I was offered the chance to come and serve as a middle school assistant principal/athletic director there, a position I eagerly accepted and grew to love as well.

I was an assistant principal for three years and can honestly say it was the most fun I have ever had as a professional. I was able to regularly interact with kids, was able to dabble in curriculum development, and cut my teeth as a change agent. While serving in my AP/AD role I decided to go back to college again and earned my Doctorate degree. While in that program I made new connections, gained new understandings, and continued to grow as a person and professional.

Two weeks after presenting my dissertation I was again presented with an offer I could not refuse. I was contacted by a woman who had been my doctoral program cohort asking me to come to her district, where she served as a central office administrator, and serve as a principal in one of her schools. Without actively pursuing jobs, I was offered my third promotion, an offer I again eagerly accepted. I served as a principal at that school in Michigan, again expanding my skill sets and learning from amazing people, for four years.

In the spring of 2015, however, I made the decision to move away from the harsh Michigan winters and to move closer to my family in Florida, where I was given the opportunity to lead a school with a history of need, a school unlike any I had ever worked in, a school that forever changed me as a person and a professional, and the ability to reflect and nurture my soul on the beach each night. I worked in the sunshine state for three years and am now back up in Michigan, serving as a Central Office administrator.

My resume shows a lot of transitions. It appears as though I am a job jumper and a career chaser, but that is not the case. In fact, the opposite is now true. I am a man who began his career chasing the money (that is so funny to even write now considering what a small amount it was), then attempted to knock down walls to get what I thought was my deserved opportunity. It wasn't until I was confronted with the reality that I was so busy looking ahead that I wasn't giving my all to today, that my career began to take shape. In my time as a leader, I have been named the State Administrator of the Year, the Collegiate Educator of the Year (I also serve as an adjunct professor) , and have had jobs literally handed to me, all because my mindset has changed. It is no longer about me. It is all about the students in my buildings and my ability to serve those who interact with them on a daily basis.

I have made a lot of mistakes along the way, many of which you will learn about if you keep reading, but I hope knowing a little more about my story helps you understand, in a better context, why I do what I do. This is what Bold Humility is all about. It is about being confident enough to work from your areas of strength, yet humble enough to admit your weaknesses. This is where trust comes from and how competence is cultivated.

 "The truth is I am flawed. I have lied. I have cheated. I have let people down. The good news is I am growing. It's a lot easier to steer when you are in motion."

KNOW YOUR CORE
SANTIAGO MEZA

New Principal, California, @santiagoAM115

This is my first year as a principal trying to lead a school that needs a foundation. I've been an assistant principal for four years and my CORE foundation in education is Special Education as a teacher for six years. Building Relationships has been extremely important in supporting and leading in the class with students and leading meetings with parents, teachers, and related service personnel to get each other to collaborate for one common purpose, the student. Leading as a person first, is crucial before a leader can engage as a professional because you want to build a foundation in relationships, then you will get people to collaborate for one purpose, a supportive system in or out of school. In building these foundations, always look for opportunities to serve rather than be served.

I often ask people throughout my day how they are doing and if the response is ever, "just ok," I ask a follow-up question, "what can I do to make your day great?" The response most of the time is, "UMMMM?" Because we don't usually ask follow-up questions, we just take what they say, and move on just as an acknowledgement, nothing more. If you want people to follow you, you have to be able to serve them first. A great leader listens, supports, and invests in people by being intentional in building relationships.

In building relationships, humans like to be cared for, supported, and made to feel safe. This is true for students in education and just as true for adults in the educational system. A staff member that feels cared for by being asked how he/she is doing on a deep level, will in-turn care about their environment and those around them (this starts a chain reaction of inquiry about others in the school, in caring deeply). A staff member that feels supported by being listened to and acknowledged, will in-turn support others in their environment (if they know you have their back, they will move mountains and will exceed your expectation). A staff member that feels safe in their environment, will love to come to work, be able to focus on educating students and feel safe to explore and try new things to help students learn (educational benefit all the way around for the students, the school, and the community).

When you build these relationships on a human level, people get to know you and the CORE you that you represent.

Those that know you as a person first, know you will support them, engage with them, and relate to them before anything is expected of them and they will seek to support you and engage with you as a person first which then translates into professional respect. If you want people to follow you and work alongside you, you have to care deeply and genuinely. Otherwise, it's just surface care and you'll get basic surface answers and work.

BOLD NEXT STEPS

1. Find a colleague that you trust and ask for explicit feedback. Ask if your passions are evident. Can others see what makes you tick?

2. Update your resume and submit it to your spouse. Ask if you were unknown to him/her, would this actually highlight your strengths.

3. Can you answer, "Was today a good day or a bad day?" What do you use as your measuring stick?

BOLD REFLECTIONS

CHAPTER TWO

ARE YOU PREPARING STUDENTS FOR THEIR FUTURES OR YOUR PAST?

I AM AN 80'S KID. I was born in 1977 and spent the bulk of my childhood in the greatest decade ever. I wore knee-high striped socks with my short shorts. I listened to Michael Jackson, Tiffany, and Guns and Roses. My beloved Detroit Pistons were winning championships and the Detroit Tigers were World Series champions. My childhood was filled with kickball, bike rides, and Mr. Wizard.

Today I have 4 children of my own. My oldest child, almost a teenager wears shorts that fall below his knees. My kids watch tv shows that they download from the internet. Kickball has been replaced by Fortnite, and my favorite sports teams probably won't even make the playoffs this year. My childhood was a long time ago and a lot has changed since then. As a child I had no internet, no home computer, no clue what my future would hold. I believed I would grow up to be a truck driver, a meteorologist, and a Navy Seal. Today, my kids dream of being vloggers and YouTube stars. My kids have no idea what childhood was like forty years ago and forty years ago I could never have imagined what childhood would look like today. Similarly, forty years ago I had no idea what adulthood would like when I actually got there, and neither did any of the adults I surrounded myself with.

Many of us have heard the statistics about the number of jobs that will exist twenty years from now that aren't even ideas in people's heads today. The reality is, we have no idea how many new jobs will exist because we have no idea what new technologies will be developed, what new consumer demands will be created, and what services will be required. Knowing all of this uncertainty exists, we as educators still try to put a sales pitch on in our classrooms telling our students why all of the content we are exposing them to is important and how it will help them in their future. Yet, all we are doing is telling these students, children with uncertain futures, how that content has helped prepare us for our present, which may or may not be relevant to their future. It is important for us to ask ourselves daily, "Are we preparing students for their futures or for our past?"

As educators, our job is to contribute to the future. We have jobs that others try to measure in moments of time through daily observations and summative assessments, even though our success can only be measured in generations. If what we are presenting to our students cannot endure, we must ask if it is something we should be spending our time on at all. Now, don't get me wrong. Standards based learning is key to achieving success. Clearly articulating objectives, assessing based on growth and progress, mastery and proficiency are all critical components of lasting learning and enduring education, but none are the silver bullet. I have built my professional reputation, my career on articulating the importance and relevance of focused standards based learning and grading, but even I know that SBL, as it is often described, is only A piece of the puzzle, not THE piece.

In education, we are often guilty of seeking the Holy Grail and Magic Pill to cure all and fix what others perceive to be broken. We attend a conference and hear one educator tell a story of what has worked in her classroom, with her kids, in her community and jump on board to try and replicate that program in our school with our kids in our way and expect the same results. We chase programs over people. We search for curriculum over creativity. When we don't see immediate results, we drift back to the status quo and wonder if the next blog we read, the next professional development seminar we attend, or the next team meeting will reveal the answer we have been looking for. We need to stop looking for THE answer and instead continue to look for AN answer, realizing that we have millions of children in a multitude of environments, with countless unknown futures who all require something a little bit different.

I currently work in a state that has adopted College and Career Readiness Standards. We believe our work in the K-12 system is to try and prepare our students for success beyond our schools. This is such a great idea, yet one so often misapplied and misinterpreted by the very people responsible for their implementation.

Times Have Changed

I am currently in my twentieth year as a professional educator. When I look back on my first year and compare it to this year, I can honestly say I was a mess when I began. Even though I didn't know it then, I can look back and definitively say, I had no idea what I was doing almost two decades ago. Prior to becoming a teacher I attended a great teacher prep university, Central Michigan University (Go, Fire Up, Chips!!), had a diverse student teaching experience, and was offered a phenomenal mentor as well, but despite all of that, when I began I was not fully prepared for the challenges I would experience. I may have thought I was, but I was so wrong. The only thing that could properly prepare me for my career was my career.

We all recognize the importance job-embedded experience has on job performance. This is why veteran teachers make more money than first-year teachers. We tend to believe that because they have had more experiences and opportunities to refine and grow their skill sets they may be more prepared to effectively perform their job duties. We understand that experience in the career is what prepares us for the career. This isn't just true in teaching. It is true in virtually every job or career you can imagine, whether it is a fry cook at a local fast food restaurant or an accountant on Wall Street. Whether you have a career in professional sports, education, engineering, public safety, or medicine, often the only thing that truly makes you ready for your career is the career...and a lot of grace offered by those you work with as you make mistakes along the way. In K-12 education, we so often lose sight of this and try to convince students, and ourselves, that by simply completing courses in our predesignated sequence, learning a bunch of facts and regurgitating information, that students will be prepared for the real world.

It's not just that we think memorizing information will help students as they grow up and enter the workforce. We tend to think it will prepare them for college too. When I look back on my first year of college, I wonder how in the world I am still alive. I graduated high school with a 3.8 G.P.A.. I was the Student Council president. I competed in sports and Model United Nations. I was a self-described model high school student, yet my first year of college was a disaster. The only thing that helped me find success and graduate from college was my ability to make it through my first year of college. I may have had some book smarts when I entered, but I was lacking a lot of "not so common" sense. I was a disaster. I entered my freshman year on an academic scholarship and started my sophomore year on the verge of academic probation.

When we say that we are preparing students to be ready for college and career are we measuring this based upon their ability to have short term retention of academic facts or are we really providing them with skills and opportunities that will transcend the safety of their K-12 school system and lead them towards long term success, regardless of what the future holds? Are we giving them the persistence, confidence, humility, and curiosity that will lead to future learning or are we giving students the answers to questions that exist today without the ability to question the answers that will exist tomorrow?

Aside from my role as a public school administrator, I also currently serve as an adjunct professor for a teacher prep college in the Midwest. I get the opportunity to take high school graduates, give them foundational understanding, and try to set them up for a long career. The college students I work with come from a wide range of communities, families, and school systems. They all had to apply for their college admissions and all were accepted, despite having a variety of past experiences. The college admissions office asks students, in their application packet, to submit, ACT scores, GPAs, transcripts, essays, records of philanthropic service, as well as descriptions of extra-curricular achievements.

Colleges understand that they should not accept students simply because of a single data point or high school transcripts. They understand that people are not defined by one test, by one grade, or by one statistic. We are who we are because of a collection of moments and experiences.

As educators we must get back to embracing that if we are indeed trying to set our students up for success in their careers and college, we are not just in the test prep business; we are in the experience creating business. Yes, we want students to learn, but real learning, learning that lasts, has nothing to do with memorizing facts and figures. Learning that lasts is all about making memories and creating experiences. Great teachers recognize this and great leaders encourage this.

As I write this, it is winter break in my school district. Kids are at home with their families, playing with new toys, attending holiday parties, and enjoying the festivities of the season. Teachers are sleeping in, sipping coffee, and trying to recover from an exhausting first half of the school year. As I write this I am projecting myself forward trying to envision five months into the future and attempting to predict what the end of the school year will look like. I feel the pressure to have high student achievement, to improve my school accountability scores, and to make my community proud of the work we are doing. This pressure is a definite reality of the educational world we now live in. I know my teachers will also feel this same pressure as spring approaches and they will feel the desire to perform, or more specifically have their students perform well on end-of-year exams and state assessments. I get it. That struggle is real and so is the pressure associated with it.

I know teachers are doing all they can. They are looking for innovative approaches to increase student success rates. They want to have more students labeled proficient. They want to score learning gains. They want their students to succeed, not just because their professional evaluations are tied to achievement results, but because they know that success this year for a child will result in a greater chance of future success.

It's Not About the Slide

The summer slide has been discussed in schools across the country for the last few years as one of the major obstacles for educators to overcome if we are ever going to be able to reach the lofty academic achievement goals that are set before us. Teachers every spring begin to throw up their hands in frustration believing that so much of what they have taught over the course of the year will be lost over the 70+ days of summer vacation and kids will slide back to where they were months before. Each fall teachers can be heard grumbling about the fact that they have to begin the year with so much review because students enter their rooms having forgotten nearly everything presented to them the year before.

Some teachers are fighting back against this by killing summer fun, family vacations, and student innate curiosity by sending home worksheet packets, summer reading lists, and workbooks. They have a belief that by keeping kids' minds busy doing these tasks in the summer, students will be fresh and ready to go when the new school year comes around as opposed to actually giving students downtime and the ability to learn, reflect, grow, and play. The irony is that it is often the same teachers who assign summer packets who say to their administrator, "I don't check my email at home because that is my time and I need time to rest and recover."

Too often we think that giving children the chance to be kids and truly explore the world around them and refine their passions without the strict guidance of mundane teacher-directed tasks is a waste of time. We think learning can only happen if we are in charge of it. Not only are our students being given way too much homework during the school year, but we are now beginning to miss the mark in the summer.

Now is a good time for me to state that I believe the summer slide is real. It has been proven through countless studies to be a reality. I believe that the problem, though, has little to do with our students, their inability to focus during the summer, or their ability to keep their minds fresh. The fault is actually ours.

As I look into the future, towards the spring, when all of the "big tests" are going to be given, Christmas Day will be 150 days in the past.

The time period between now and the "big test" is approximately twice as long as the 77 days that comprise a typical summer vacation. Even 150 days from now, I would bet that if I were to ask any of my students in May if they could remember Christmas Day, a day that by then would be five months in the past, the vast majority would be able to describe for the gifts they received, the time they woke up, maybe even the weather outside. They would be able to describe in detail, a day that occurred five months in the past. I have strong doubts, however, about how many students would be able to remember the content learned from the extra homework packet that was sent home with them over winter break.

The issue has nothing to do with whether a child has enough worksheets or books to read to maintain their memories (my own kids have done no Christmas related worksheets or read any Christmas books since December 25th). The issue is that Christmas Day was made to be an event. It was not presented to kids as a task, a lesson, or something to be memorized like so much of our school-based instruction. It was made into a memory unlike so much that we try to get kids to memorize.

Because we live in an age of so much accountability in schools, educators everywhere are working extremely hard to introduce students to new content as quickly as possible. We begin to think that in order to bring about testing success, we must fill every moment of every day with homework, worksheets, workbooks, quizzes, and tests. By the time the "big tests" arrive, at the end of the school year, students have such fatigue that success doesn't come. Then during the final days of the school year, when we could be celebrating another milestone completed, teachers decide to double down on our efforts to try and avoid the same stress and disappointment the following year by sending home summer packets to prepare students for the next school year and attempt to avoid the infamous summer slide.

The following fall students will arrive back to school after completing the summer packet, take a pre-assessment that still shows a regression of learning, and the panic will begin to grow again. More homework will be assigned each night during that school year and the cycle will repeat itself again This pattern of behavior is often encouraged and endorsed by leaders, with the best of intentions, both explicitly, and implicitly by their own actions towards their teachers and staff.

In life, we learn by watching than by doing. Babies do not learn how to walk and talk by sitting in a small group and being directed to proper step cadence and annunciation. They watch adults walking and talking and they attempt to mimic, failing often at first, and quickly improving on their way to mastery. A child does not learn to ride his bike by sitting behind a desk receiving a lecture on the purpose of the spokes, seat, handlebars, and brakes. Their curiosity is aroused by watching others do it and then they hop on and try it themselves. They receive guidance, encouragement, and support. This is the way learning and mastery happens. It is only in the artificial environment of schools that we treat initial struggles as failures and slap labels on individuals who do not conform to the norm.

We do this, often, not because we have any pedagogical basis, but because doing so makes our jobs easier. It allows us to respond to kids in the same way we were responded to in school years ago. We think that it is our responsibility to place hoops in front of kids to earn their right to an education by jumping through the same ritualistic education that we did as kids as though it is a rite of passage that we all have to endure. Our job is not to make kids endure school, but to encourage them to embrace learning. Your job as an educator is to give kids balance, not to push them over.

I was a classroom teacher for eight years and have been a school administrator for more than a decade. I understand accountability and the need to monitor student achievement. It is vital to ensuring successful schools and systems. When I began my career in the state of Michigan, teachers were asked to give up three weeks of instruction in the fall to provide the state summative assessment. That's right, in the fall. The reason, as explained by state-level educational experts, behind that system was to afford the state ample time to analyze results and share them with relevant stakeholders during the school year. Assessing students later in the school year did not provide the same "luxury". After years of debate about the validity of a fall assessment, the state changed its system, believing, as many educators do today, that assessing learning after the summer months is not an accurate measure of learning. After all, how can we possibly expect students to remember all that we have taught them last year after three months of playing outside and not doing all of our assigned homework and worksheets? Many believe, if we are going to give state assessments, the only way to accurately measure learning is if we measure it near the end of an academic year like we now do in virtually every state, with a spring summative, big stakes assessment.

Let's Get Kids to Upload More Than They Download

It is important to remember, however, our job as educators is not to teach kids skills that will last until the end of a school year. Our job is to prepare kids for life, a life beyond school, a life without us, a life that is still unknown, a life that they are living now and will live in the future. What good is it to test students on skills we expect them to master in the spring if we are willing to admit they will not remember them even a few months later after living in the real world and out of the artificial fishbowl of our classrooms.

As educators, our job is not to create lessons, but to establish memories. We need to stop saying that we teach content and begin to embrace learning that lasts, education that endures. It's Like Riding a Bike- it really is. We have all heard the saying "Once you learn how to ride a bike, you never forget." This is so true. Even if you haven't hopped on a bike in years, if you learned as a child, you can get on a bike tomorrow and go for a ride around the block. The learning you acquired when mastering this skill has endured. This is lasting learning at its finest. Memories last. Lessons are forgotten.

As educators, our job is to create learners, not copycats. Most of us get that. In classrooms, we put procedures in place to inhibit student cheating. We say we want students to produce original work. On test day we tell students to use a cover sheet, to move desks so that they are not seated next to each other, and we monitor for wandering eyes. We want to make sure that students are not stealing the ideas of their peers, yet at the same time, we are 100% OK if students copy our words. Why are we OK with students writing down our every word in class and then simply spitting them back to us to show mastery of a topic, but we cringe when thinking a student may do the same thing with a peer. The hypocrisy is real. We say "no" to cheating when a kid copies a kid, but celebrate it when a kid copies us.

We take it a step further when we do our own interpretation of one of the most "popular" English Language Arts standards being taught to kids today. Every state in America has a standard similar to this. We teach students to use text to learn and then to ask them to "cite textual evidence" to prove an answer to a question. The intent is to have students base opinions and insights on fact, to find established evidence to support claims, but what we are often teaching students is that as long as an adult has put an idea into print or a teacher has made a statement to a class, it must be the truth.

Teachers, our job is not to create compliant students who can spit back information, but instead to create learners who actively question answers in search of new truths to challenge the thinking of the status quo. If we really want a better world, we have to allow students the freedom to question the realities of our current world.

The fault is not with teachers, though. It's bigger than that. We are all the products of our environments. We all have employers who set goals, objectives, and agendas. Teachers do what they do because of their attempt to live up to the expectations of those put into authority over them. In America today there are more than 90,000 public school principals. The vast majority began their careers as classroom teachers. It is reasonable to assume these principals found some measure of success in their classrooms that led them to pursue advancement. As a result, when principals move into their new roles many erroneously seek, hire, and train teachers who will provide instruction in a manner that resembles what they used to provide in their own classrooms. After all, if it was good enough for them, it must be good enough for others.

This is the same mindset so many parents bring with them to school meetings when innovative new approaches are discussed by the rare school leader willing to try and break the mold. They are often challenged by the successful parent who judges his or her child's current school by comparing it to the same system they encountered decades earlier when they were a part of it. The pressure to conform to the way things have always been becomes so strong that often the cycle just continues. Unfortunately, our students suffer, and we become more and more entrenched as we prepare students for our own system, not the real world of the future.

As a leader, I know I have a distinct charge. I am a part of the system that I am trying to change. I understand that all great changes in society have resulted from grassroots movements from the inside. I cannot simply complain about the way things are and wait for an outside force to step in and drive the change I want to happen. I need to be the change. That does not mean my job is to develop innovative strategies and processes and then impose them on my staff. That defeats the purpose. I don't want anyone to simply copy what I am doing or saying. I want everyone to play their own part.

I am a firm believer that if I can get others to weigh in, I will not have to work to get buy-in. My job is to hire the best then get out of the way. The single most important responsibility I have is to hire amazing people who are willing to reflect, to grow, and to change. I need people with the required certifications and qualifications, but more importantly, I need people with the right heart. I need people who can answer the question "Has it been a good day or a bad day?" I need people who have a purpose and a mission and know how to articulate why they do what they do. I need people who are willing to question me, their peers, and themselves. It is only through a reflective culture, a culture of quiet confidence, a culture of collaboration and honest self-assessment, a culture of growth and improvement, that an environment of Bold Humility can begin to be fostered and developed, and this is where the magic happens.

As an administrator, I have to further the conversations that matter to me. Taboo topics only exist in cultures that cherish the status quo. If I allow and engage in public conversations about our most sacred educational traditions, the teachers that work with me will feel the freedom to do the same. The only way to foster change is to acknowledge that there may be better ways to do things. If we want our students to grow and change the world, teachers must model it, and they will only do so if their principals do the same. Be the change to see the change.

 "We don't ask kids to label the parts of their bike before we help them get on and learn to ride. 'It's Like Riding a Bike: How to make learning last a lifetime' Once you learn how, you never forget!"

LIVE FREE
JENNIFER QUATTRUCCI

Elementary School Teacher, Rhode Island, @jenquattrucci

I believe that in a world where children are rushed from place to place, often on devices, we need to create an environment where they are given time and allowed to focus, to think, to create and to learn. I've always wanted to be a teacher. I can remember being five years old in kindergarten and going home and setting up my stuffed animals and dolls to play school. I would read them the stories my father read to me. I would draw and paint and create shoe box dioramas and mobiles based on the stories I loved. My mother and father both encouraged my love of literature. My dad took me and my sister to the library quite often and my mom would sew outfits based on storybook characters for me and sometimes even for my dolls.

As I got older I remained an avid reader and always loved learning, but what I enjoyed most of all was working with young children. I loved helping them learn and seeing them smile when they enjoyed a story or special activity. I spent a great deal of time with my younger cousins and they quite often became my "students" as we read and discovered different topics to explore. We experimented with cooking, baking, making up games, taking apart toys, and just having fun researching different topics with our World Book Encyclopedias.

This is how I still teach today. I have been teaching in the inner city of Providence, Rhode Island for more than 23 years. I try my best to provide an atmosphere where children are excited about learning and are allowed to learn at their own pace. Our activities and learning experiences are hands-on, developmentally appropriate, literature based, and inspire authentic learning. I have a forthcoming book which includes 180 screen-free, hands-on, creative ideas and lesson plans for classroom teachers of students PreK-Grade 6, called (working title) Educate the Heart: Screen-Free Activities for Grades Prek-6 to Inspire Authentic Learning in Your Classroom. It includes ideas for collaborative art projects, proper ways to encourage mathematical discourse, STEM challenges, literacy center ideas, author study favorites and so much more! I hope my book will inspire educators to make the most of their time with their amazing students so we as a teaching community can continue to create meaningful moments and provide students with the skills, support, and confidence they need to become their best selves!

BOLD NEXT STEPS

1. Make a list of the 5 things you love about your school or classroom, the five things you would want to see replicated anywhere by anyone. Then identify two things in your school or class that get in the way of you meeting your professional goals. Schedule a time with your direct supervisor to discuss both lists and what to do with them.

2. During your next classroom lesson, staff meeting, or professional development opportunity, identify three people to assist you in growing. One person will calculate how much time you spend talking during the session. One person will calculate the number of questions you ask others to answer. One person will calculate the number of different people you engage with. Have them turn these stats in once the session is complete. Just knowing others are doing this will give you an awareness, but each time you share, work to improve in each area.

3. Make a personal connection with each person you learn with. Keep a journal identifying their passions and interests. Before engaging with them in the future, study what you know, find ways to bring it up, and work to increase your knowledge of them. The more you learn about them, the more they will learn from you.

BOLD REFLECTIONS

CHAPTER THREE

LIFE ON THE CATWALK

MY INSTAGRAM, Twitter, and Facebook feeds are filled with pictures of my kids. To know me is to know my kids. I mean it. My kids are just like me. They are good looking, funny, smart, and have tremendous charisma. I'm joking, kind of. As each of my children grow up, I find myself increasingly being hit over the head with reflections of who I am. Lucky for each of them, they have not acquired my physical appearance yet, but my mannerisms, habits, and words are popping out of them with greater regularity. Who I am is who they are becoming. They learn more from watching me than they do from listening to my rants and raves. They mimic me because I am the closest thing to a successful adult in their world. I see it when they play. I hear it when they speak. Sometimes it makes me smile with pride, and sometimes it makes me cringe in humility.

As a dad, my challenge to myself is to try and be the person I want my boys to be and to act like the man I want my daughter to marry. That is a large burden to carry, but it is one that, whether I accept it or not, will be my reality. This is the reason I date my daughter. I want to model for her what to expect from a gentleman. This is the reason I say "Please" and "Thank you" to my sons. It is the reason I rise early in the morning and work out daily. It is the reason I read in front of them and not in a secluded corner. I know I am a model for their present and future behavior, and it is the perfect accountability to make me better each day.

At work, I have amazing principals, teachers, secretaries, custodians, and students. Every single one of the people I work with makes my life better and I am so grateful. These are not just words being written. These are genuine words of appreciation and gratitude. I know that my life has been impacted by the people I work with because they are special, unique, and driven.

As a leader, I know my responsibility is not just to help craft and draft a mission statement, write policy, and sign checks. Every single day I work with other adults who are watching my every move, even when I don't notice it. They watch to see if there are signs of discouragement or signs of hope. They watch to see if I will offer a hug to a struggling student or walk right by. They watch to see if I will extend grace to a teacher who overslept or if I will correct with consequences.

My job is to model to the adults, what I expect the adults to display to the children in their care. If I say that it is essential that every child walks into a room knowing they are safe and loved, I must make the time to ensure every staff member feels the same way. If I expect every teacher to articulate goals and objectives to their students, I must take the time daily to do the same for my teachers. If I expect every expectation to be explicitly taught, I must remember that even to adults, sometimes what we should know by now is not what we do know now.

In my last year as a building principal I had the following goals for myself: Pass out at least 50 hugs a day, visit at least 30 classrooms a week, make at least 100 parent phone calls a month, smile at every person I pass in the hall, get out from behind my desk each time I have a conversation in my office, start every workday with a full staff huddle before the kids arrive, and display hope and optimism in each conversation I have. Those were my goals because I expected my teachers to get to know their students, to provide love and guidance, to be explicit in their expectations, and to remember that the life-changing business is a good business. I wanted my teachers to get out from behind their desks, to articulate their vision, and to teach with kindness.

I Make Mistakes...and So Do You

As a leader, no job or responsibility is beneath me. My job is to dress up in costumes, to make a caricature of myself daily, to pick up trash, to fill in for absent teachers, to serve others, and lead by example. My example will say more than my words ever will and it is this personal challenge of mine that will help teachers change the lives of kids.

Leaders- yes you have to balance budgets, do evaluations, supervise bus duty, and deal with disgruntled parents, but you know what...so do your teachers. If you want your teachers to lead the next generation with love and inspiration, in spite of the stress and burdens that surround them, then lead your teachers the same way. Teachers, the same wisdom goes for you. You must act the way you want your students to act. You must demonstrate what you expect. Model what you want. Yes, I know you are not a student. I know the same rules should not apply to you as they do to your students. Yes, I know you can vote, drink, smoke, and drive. I know you are old enough to make your own decisions and live your own life, but one of the decisions that you made was to accept your part in shaping the lives of the kids who are watching your every move. When you chose to enter into this "most noble" of professions, the bar was raised. You chose this career and along with it the responsibility that comes with it. Your students notice when you roll your eyes at that kid who shows up late. They hear the complaining spilling out of the teachers' lounge. They recognize your car on the street and see you rolling through that stop sign in town. Right or wrong, they are watching.

This pressure can get intense, but don't let it get the best of you. Our students also need to see us make mistakes, apologize for them, and recover. They need to see that we are human and need to see what responsible adults do when they make mistakes. This does not, however, give us the right to act however we want or to put ourselves on a pedestal in front of our students.

As educators, I think that we often get it wrong. In our attempts to help prepare our students for adulthood we make the claim that we are trying to teach our students what the "real world" looks like forgetting that our students are living in a world that is very real today. We use this claim to give ourselves an excuse to treat our students in the way that some of us have been treated by employers in the past, erroneously thinking that just because there are bad bosses in the world, we have to equip our students to deal with them someday. We forget that our job is to empower students to see the world for what it could be, instead of what it has been. Because of this, schools often become the breeding ground for oxymoronic behavior. If you are guilty of any of the following, feel free to humble yourself and call yourself an oxyMORON, then have the boldness to change.

Focus on Priority Over Preference

For example, have you ever been sitting around the dinner table with your family and notice you have an incoming call or text from your boss. Instead of answering it you make the statement. "Doesn't he realize I work all day for him? This is my time to be with my family." You flip the phone upside down and continue to enjoy quality time at home. The next day you go to your classroom, teach all day, and then assign homework for students to complete that evening after they have been sitting through seven hours of content, social skill building, and potentially two more hours of physical activity. You hear their grumbles about their busy schedules as you assign it, but reply with "It should take (less than the time it would have taken you to answer the call the night before). Just get it done." You wouldn't take a couple of minutes out of "your time" the night before to do work from your boss, but you expect kids to?!

It is always fascinating to me that some teachers are OK with a kid missing family time to do schoolwork, yet get upset when a kid misses school to do family time. You know what I am talking about. You assign that big project or test. You provide students with weeks of advance notice and you still get that student that comes to you the day before it's due with the list of excuses about why he needs an extension. You explain the need to be organized and use time at home wisely to get schoolwork done and deny the request. The following month, a different child approaches and explains that he is hoping to go on vacation for a week and needs his schoolwork to complete while gone. Knowing how inconvenient this is to YOU, you greet this student with the same sighs and lectures as the student with the list of excuses the month before.

I know kids should be in school. I know teachers are facilitators of learning activities and provide the best path for students to learn academic content. That does not dismiss the irony of the situation though. We complain that parents are not involved in the lives of their kids when we see their kids as students, but complain when they step in to become memory makers. We cannot say hands-on, relevant learning opportunities matter, and then get frustrated when a parent decides to step up and create an experience for their child. We cannot get frustrated at our school or district when funds are not available for more field trips and then blame a parent for designing their own. We cannot take days out of our curriculum to show movies, to take field trips to amusement parks, to have field days, and pep rallies, and then tell a parent that their ideas for enrichment have less value than ours. Teachers and leaders, we cannot get away with a do as I say not as I do attitude. Followers will always do what we do. Always!

When I was a classroom teacher I was as guilty of this as anyone. I was unbending, inflexible, and rigid. I expected my students to study to learn and to do it on their own time. It wasn't until a few years ago, when I was presenting to a group of strangers that I made a statement that hit me across the face and made me realize that I was that same hypocrite I was complaining about.

I had just finished a discussion about standards-based grading and the importance of timely feedback. As always, at the end of my presentation, I allowed the audience to ask questions to refine their thinking. I don't remember the exact questions that were asked, but I know they dealt with the relevance of testing, when to give them, if they should be given, and how much value they should have. The line of questions led me to make the following statements. "How do you know when your students are ready for a test? If you know they are ready, why do you need to test them? If you don't know that they are ready, is it fair to test them? Furthermore, if a student is not ready, who is responsible for making them ready? If a student can learn it all on his own, what is the purpose of a teacher? If a student has to study for a test, is a teacher even needed?" Yup, I was on a roll. Through a series of questions and answers, related to a presentation I had given dozens of times, I was beginning to articulate and refine a belief that I had never really explicitly stated before.

Through this exchange, one message was emerging. Teachers matter more. Teachers matter more than programs, processes, or procedures. Teachers must embrace that they are responsible for student learning. We cannot say student learning requires a textbook, more technology, or even a student's ability to study. Sure, these may all make the job easier, but teachers matter more. As a principal, my job was not to be on the hunt for the next best curriculum enhancement, program, or gimmick, but instead to ensure that my teachers recognized the tremendous power they have in determining the destinies of their students.

We speak to our students about relevance, working hard to make connections from our content to their future, but the reality is, kids are already working to make associations. They are studying us as people as much, if not more than, they are studying the content we are presenting them. If schools are supposed to be microcosms of society, it is our obligation to make sure the processes and practices we put into place represent the hope we have for the future. I hope to play a part in helping to create people who value people. I hope to create people who understand that time is a gift. I hope to create people who are smart, kind, and loving. I hope to create people who are strong, independent, and decisive. I hope to create people who are innovative and creative. I hope to create people who are "compassionate, honest, focused, cheerful, curious, diplomatic, flexible, bold, and humble."

If you watch any of the superhero movies that are popular today, you will notice that the villain is often the smartest character. Simply giving students content knowledge is a stepping stone, but creating good people with the knowledge to collaborate and make decisions is what we need in order to help create heroes.

To do this, I believe we must address a few practices that may seem trivial to us, but actually say a whole lot to our kids.

Home Time is a Time to Reflect and Plan...For Us and For Them

Earlier I mentioned my favorite interview question to ask when hiring a staff member, "How do you know if it has been a good day or a bad day?" The goal of this question is to help me and my committee determine how reflective a candidate is. The ability to accurately reflect is often what separates mediocre from excellent. Reflection is what leads to growth and what allows us to improve. Many of us have heard of Bloom's Taxonomy where we analyze the depth of learning. Designed by Benjamin Bloom more than fifty years ago, this framework articulates that the creation of new or original work is the epitome of high order thinking. I do not disagree, but in the *Schmittou Revised Edition*, I would argue that reflection is a level above. It is great to be able to evaluate the creation of someone else. It is great to be able to use your knowledge to create something original that is even better, but it is an even richer experience to create something you think is amazing, evaluate it yourself, then make it even better. This is what reflection is all about, and this is a skill we could all benefit from practicing more regularly.

As a runner, I understand the need for "off days". These are the days where I simply rest my muscles and my joints so that they can regenerate and actually come back stronger. One of the leading causes of injury for athletes stems from overuse, as we do not give our bodies the time needed to really grow and develop so we break down. As a matter of fact, before I run a marathon, I will take 10 days off from any running at all. The same strategy is needed with our mental muscles. We need time to grow. We need down time where our minds are able to reflect on the hard work of the day so that we can come back stronger the next day. For some, this means taking time to be with family. Some binge watch TV shows. I like to spend time alone on the beach. Whatever your method of taking downtime, we all need it. It is needed for our students as well. It is needed every day. It is needed every year. It is needed with frequency. Overworking, although it may sound like a way to be more productive, often leads to more harm than good. Imagine what would happen if the two weeks before the big state test this spring, you told students not to study, not to work on school at home, but just to relax. It goes against what we feel like we should be doing, but it may be just the game changer your kids need.

I am not going to get on my soapbox and preach against homework. That has been done already, but I will add this one sentence for you to reflect on. The teacher who assigns homework simply to promote a strong work ethic should have a strong enough work ethic to find another way. Discussing the relevance of assigned work, both classwork and homework is a personal passion of mine, but it is not the hill for me to die on now. What I will advocate for is for us to make sure we are affording our students the time to not just practice their content knowledge, but their people skills as well. Give them time to play (no matter their age). Give them time to socialize, cooperate, and engage. As a father, I know that my children will benefit more from one on one time with me at the dinner table than they will from filling out another set of flashcards in their bedroom to prepare for a test filled with information they will forget in a week. As a leader, I know my teachers will come back to work tomorrow stronger and more mentally sound, ready to successfully handle the turmoil involved in the day to day of teaching if they are given the chance to breathe and relax at home this evening. Barring an emergency, I do my best not to send emails after 5pm. I would rather my teachers have the chance to eat dinner with their families than feel the need to check their phone or computer all night to answer a question from me that can probably wait until the morning. The truth of the matter is that we all want to please our bosses. Even in those moments when we get that text or email at home, we spend a minute debating whether or not we should reply. If you are like me, maybe you even spend a few seconds every couple of minutes just looking for notifications of incoming messages on your phone. It is constant. This distraction is just enough to help you disengage from your quiet downtime and get you back into burning mental energy.

I will be honest. I am not as good at this practice as I hope others are. My phone is practically glued to my hand as I anticipate an urgent message from someone at almost all hours of the day, but this does not mean I have to perpetuate this cycle to those who report to me. If I get an email from a teacher or principal, after hours, unless it is an absolute emergency, odds are I will not respond until the following day. I can almost guarantee that I will read the message within minutes of receiving it, but I will not reply. This isn't because I am trying to be rude, but because I am trying to model the expectation. I will find that teacher or principal first thing the next morning and reply in person, explaining my desire for them to disconnect while at home. I do not want anyone to feel the need to sit by and wait in anticipation for an online dialogue with me. I am not more important than anyone in anyone's family.

Don't Ever Meet to Meet

Many school systems across the country have mandatory seat time requirements for students. I understand the intent behind these policies. We know students as a whole, perform better when they are sitting in a classroom receiving instruction from a qualified, certified, educational professional. Why is this a requirement, though? Is it because some students feel that their class doesn't add value so showing up isn't needed? Is it because some students were showing success without attending class? If this is the case, there may be other issues to discuss. Is it because some students were struggling in class, stopped showing up and we felt the need to punish the student who didn't show success by giving another form of condemning feedback? The truth of the matter is if a student knows he/she will be engaged at a high level and understands that real, lasting, enduring knowledge will come from attending class regularly, whether there is a seat time requirement or not, the vast majority will choose to show up. Sure, there will be some that will choose to disengage, but those are the outliers and should not drive the norm.

What if at your school, you were the best teacher around. I mean, the data proved it, your observations proved it, and your students knew it. You taught standing on your head, students signed up in droves to be in your class, and yet at the end of the year, you were given an evaluation score that showed you were an ineffective teacher because you failed to show up for required staff meetings. It doesn't matter that each staff meeting was simply a review of the calendar that you already had access to online, along with the principal reading PowerPoint slides to you that could have simply been shared electronically. It doesn't matter that the meetings were held after school and you were a coach for an athletic team and just couldn't be there. Your evaluation rubric indicated that your attendance was a requirement and there was no way around it, regardless of the lack of relevance or need. The meetings were a waste of time and everyone knew it. Most of us would probably challenge a policy like this, and rightly so.

If it's not good for you as an adult, it's probably not good for them as a student.

Keep it Private

What if that same evaluation that you received showing where you were "deficient" was made public for the world to see? I know, because of privacy laws we are not allowed to share private personnel issues, nor are we supposed to share student grade information, but some still do. In an attempt to make an example of students, we put students and their work on display for others to see. Sometimes we do it to highlight success and sometimes it is to condemn failure. Maybe you aren't as blatant as to explicitly shame a student publicly, but...

- Do you have a clip chart and ask students to take a walk of shame to the front of the room and change it when they make a poor decision?

- Do you group kids in homogeneous groups, where "smart kids" and "slow kids" work with like peers, obvious to everyone?

- Do you create homogeneous classes, like Intervention and Advanced based upon labels "earned" in previous years?

- Do you have a "silent lunch" table for students who are being separated from their peers due to social skill struggles?

- Do you put "exemplary" work on display while others have their work returned?

The messages we send to kids are not always explicit, but they are always received. What would happen if at your next staff meeting all teachers were split into groups based on their IQ scores? What would happen if at your next staff meeting teachers who were playing on their phones, having sidebar conversations, or arrived late were asked to walk to the front of the room and move their clips? What if at your staff Christmas Party, several teachers were told not to attend due to poor performance or were asked to sit at a table and watch the party from afar because during the school year they had a few social struggles? If we treated adults the way we sometimes treat students we would be appalled.

We try to frame some of these decisions as "holding students accountable" or try to justify our actions because "the good kids need to see that we have a high standard", but would any excuse be a good excuse to treat adults like this? Sure, there may be a few sadistic staff members out there that relish in seeing their peers finally called out, but I can guarantee, having practices in place like this will not enhance the workplace culture. It will create a culture of compliance, not collaboration. We will see fear and not value. We need to work to elevate everyone, adults, staff, and ourselves. Our goal should always be to repair, renew, and recharge, never to deflate, diminish, or disparage.

Don't Let Others Make a Fool of You. Do it Yourself.

I have spent the bulk of my career in middle schools, and I have learned that working with middle schoolers is really not that different from working with kindergarten students or high school freshmen. If you do not love them, they will eat you up and spit you out. For those of you who have never worked in a middle school before, let me tell you what middle school students are really like. They are weird. They are bizarre. They crave attention and individuality. They want to be accepted yet want to be original. They are loud, extroverted caricatures of children of all ages. Kids of all ages, from 0-100, crave relationships. We want to be with and around people who are real, people who are honest, genuine, and passionate.

I guarantee most of us would be taken aback if we learned that our best friend went on a blind date last night and came home engaged. We would argue that the new couple should take some time to get to know each other, because a first date is normally a place where individuals are reserved and guarded, only sharing select pieces of their full identity. We know that it is important to push through the facade and get to know the real person before making such a big commitment. As educators we are asking students to be engaged in our work, to be committed to us and trust us with their futures, yet often we do this without really letting them get to know us.

As teachers who have a desire to be relatable and to have students who can identify with us, it is our responsibility to be willing to make a fool of ourselves just as much as the students do. We can't preach to students the importance of taking a stand, the power of individuality, exerting platitudes about not always doing what's popular, while we choose to wear our same standard khakis, loafers, and a polo shirt to work every day (these aren't bad, they just aren't for everyone). We can't act as though spirit days are just for kids and expect kids to embrace our message of risk-taking and engagement. We can't encourage kids to show school spirit while we simply preach it from behind our desks.

It is our responsibility to be unique, to be creative, and inventive. Playing it safe will cause you to drown in a classroom faster than jumping into the deep end ever will. Students are daredevils as children. Before they turn five years old kids are accustomed to falling down and stumbling before getting back up and trying again as they learn to walk and talk. They are used to failing and rising again. Then they enter school and we tell them to keep taking chances while we show them a life of playing it safe. Administrators ask teachers to conform to a script when they are being evaluated and begin to believe this is what effective teaching is all about. We ask teachers to follow pacing guides and wag our finger in disapproval when every teacher in a department is not on the same page on the same day. We tell our teachers they need to differentiate for students yet we stand in front of our staff at a faculty meeting and read from a PowerPoint for an hour. If we want different, we have to be different.

This does not mean we all need to dress up in funny costumes to help teach thematic lessons. This does not mean that we as leaders begin to go against the norm and then require every teacher to do the same. If we want individualism and creativity, we have to encourage it, model, and be willing to make a fool of ourselves, doing what nobody else would ever be willing to do. When you are willing to make a fool of yourself and try something new with regularity you give permission for those who follow you to do it too, whether they are peers or students.

Coupled with the ability to reflect, creativity takes teaching to a new level. Be you. The real you and embrace it for everyone to see. Make yourself vulnerable as vulnerability is a requirement for trust. The best teachers are extremely mature with childlike personalities. Maturity is a choice, not a process. Choose to be mature enough to act like a fool from time to time. Your school culture and climate will thank you.

 "Teachers are not commodities! They are destiny shapers!"

BE WHO YOU NEEDED WHEN YOU WERE YOUNGER
JULIE STEWART

Special Ed Teacher, Florida, @onesweetbatch

Would I like to be a student in my classroom? Would I be engaged and eager to learn new things? Would I be willing to tell everyone about what happened in class that day? Teachers have a monstrous workload, but often we are missing an opportunity to make a meaningful, long-lasting impact on our students by showing them how enjoyable life with them can be.

Thinking of our own learning experiences it is sometimes difficult to pinpoint one teacher or classroom activity that really made a difference. Teachers have the enormous responsibility of reaching and teaching every student while making lessons and activities relevant and fun. Those two ideas aren't mutually exclusive. It is fundamental to have a strong classroom management plan, but equally important for students to see their teachers laugh and be playful.

Ideally, we should connect with each student on a deeper level than just surface classroom banter. I have taught second grade and college courses and every grade/subject in between in the past fifteen years. In my own classrooms, I found that the times I let my guard down, belly-laughed, and made a fool of myself were the experiences and lessons that my students took with them. Students that felt supported and understood came to class to get pumped for the remainder of their day. Students that had reputations for being not so nice were able to come to my room to be themselves. Respect is of utmost importance, and I both demanded and delivered it. If you can't enjoy what you do for 8+ hours a day, why would you expect children to?

Ideally, we want students to revel in their school experience. We spend more time with these young adults than we do our own families. It makes sense that we should be ourselves when working with them. It's okay to be messy, laugh, joke, and stay current with pop culture. Students need to see their teachers as someone they can confide in, ask advice from, and listen to. Messes can be cleaned, but the memories and conversations will remain.

My "why" is and always will be because the kids need me. There may never be another adult in their life that laughs with them, connects with them, or talks with them. Teachers have the responsibility and opportunity to truly connect with students every day - it's okay to embrace your own inner child to make that happen. Make jokes, dance, smile, ask them the important questions. Just BE with them.

BOLD NEXT STEPS

1. Challenge yourself to put your phone down when you get home from work and to leave your computer powered down tonight (unless you are participating in my Twitter chat, #LastingLearning- I can totally make an exception for that).

2. Look through the next unit of study you will be presenting to your students and identify a character you can dress up as to help make it memorable for them and you (Tangram Man? Rosie the Riveter? The Anti-bullying Bulldog? The Maître D helping to serve students at the Periodic Table?). For bonus points don't tell anyone about it until you do it, the fully embrace their "You're crazy" looks.

3. Assign your students or staff homework tonight that requires them to just sit and talk. Help them grow closer and stronger by growing as people.

BOLD REFLECTIONS

CHAPTER FOUR

IT'S NICE MEETING YOU

I WENT into a classroom the other day and observed an amazingly organized teacher. She had folders for everything. She had shelves for incoming work and shelves for outgoing work. She had her students taking attendance and had students passing out technology. To say she was efficient would be an understatement. Near the front of her room, this teacher had a folder, clipped to the whiteboard with a magnet, labeled "Absent Work." Intrigued by this, I took a closer look and found packets of worksheets labeled with student names so that those who were not in attendance that day could grab a packet when they returned. (Actually writing the names on the packets was the job of another student in class who worked alongside the attendance recorder). Although this was extremely efficient, let me say this, teachers, if all a student has to do is some make-up work when he is absent, your lesson plans may need a rewrite.

Last month I went to do some consultant work at a school in the desert southwest. The school was new, had technology galore, and was filled with a passionate energetic teaching staff. On the day of my visit I had the opportunity to speak with the building principal, observe multiple classrooms, provide feedback, and attend an after-school staff meeting. One of the celebrations that the principal of this school shared with me was that his staff meetings were no longer business meetings, they were now professional development opportunities. To culminate my visit, he wanted me to attend one of his meetings and observe the outcome. Just before walking to the cafeteria, the setting for the meeting, the principal was stopped in the hall by a teacher, a history teacher who I had observed earlier in the day. The teacher wanted to remind the principal that she would not be attending the staff meeting because she had to take her spouse to the airport that evening. The caring and understanding principal excused the teacher and said, "Just swing by my office tomorrow morning. I will give you a five-minute summary of all that we cover." Although this was extremely compassionate and generous, let me say this, principals, if you can hold a five-minute make-up staff meeting, you should have held a five-minute staff meeting.

Every Meeting is a Chance to Learn, Grow, and Reflect

In my last school, we did away with weekly staff meetings. This was in a school with extremely high needs and a historical record of being labeled an F by state accountability standards. I didn't require teachers to stay after school and listen to me share all of my wisdom. I didn't require teachers to sit and get. I grew to appreciate that teachers are exhausted at the end of the day. Once kids get on buses to head home, I didn't want my teachers to come see me and think, "Great, one more meeting." Instead, I tried to value their time so they, in turn, could feel valued. I wanted to allow teachers to have the afternoon to reflect on the day while it was still fresh. I wanted them to seek out their peers and collaborate, vent, and socialize.

I know how tired my own children are at the end of the day and the struggle I, as a parent, endure trying to motivate them to do homework beyond the school day. If I expect high quality results and high quality learning, pulling people together when they are most exhausted and asking them to be actively engaged in high level professional growth activities is probably not the best move.

In my school, the decision to eliminate staff meetings was a necessity. That school was a hard place to work. I saw first-hand the exhaustion on my teachers' faces each afternoon. If I wanted to protect them as people and avoid unnecessary burn out, I had to do something different. I could not expect them to teach students all day, to have children as their focus for 8 hours, to put out fires, to assess, to instruct, to love all day long and then expect them to be actively engaged in any staff meeting or professional development after school. At the same time, having a building with so many new teachers, due to high turnover rates, necessitated frequent and regular opportunities for professional growth. The solution, Morning Huddles.

Being a huge sports fan, I often steal both metaphors and strategies from the athletic fields and courts. One of the reasons I think I was a successful teacher is because I would often approach lesson planning the same way I would approach game planning. As a coach, my job was to find the unique skills of each player. I would develop systems based on the talents of each kid. At practice, my plans would be based on the performance of previous games. I would study film of my athletes and design drills designed to make each better, knowing that with collective individual growth, the team would grow as well.

At my school, students arrived early. We were a building where 100% of our students receive free breakfast and free lunch. We often had students waiting around before our doors opened, eager to grab the breakfast items prepared for them in the cafeteria because for far too many, the lunch we provided the day before was the last time they ate. The students piled into the building at 6:50am each morning, making a beeline for the cafeteria, grabbing their bags of breakfast, and then heading to their classrooms to spend the next fifteen minutes eating and enjoying the company and conversation of their teacher.

This was a critical time of the day. I believe positive personal relationships are key for learning. The beginning of the day is not the time for teachers to scurry around and finish their lesson plans, to make copies, or do general house cleaning. This is a time where teachers need to be present, attentive, and focused on each child. This is the time where teachers can connect with their students on a personal level, can set the stage for engagement, and make each child feel valued. To make this happen, teachers must come to work each day prepped and ready to go.

During my first two years working in that building, I often found dozens of teachers scurrying around the building from 6:30am-6:50am making copies, grading papers, and discussing last-minute plan adaptations, but for many, the scurry would rarely end at 6:50, even as kids were entering. Students would walk into their rooms, sit at their desks, begin eating and rarely be greeted or engaged by the teachers until class "officially" started at 7:10am, or beyond. Using the last ten minutes to prepare and plan was never enough and always spilled over into some of the most valuable time of the school day. Like most things, though, this was not just a teacher issue. It was a "me" issue. This was a result of my leadership and what I modeled and so, after some reflection, I decided I had to change my own daily schedule as well.

Nothing Highlights Your Priorities Quite Like Your Schedule

Each day, my cell phone wakes me up at 4am. That alarm notifies me that it is time to get up, get dressed, and go for a run on the dark streets of my neighborhood. I carry a flashlight, strap on my phone to my arm, lace my shoes, and put three to five miles on my feet every morning. Do I like waking up this early? No, I actually hate it. Do I like running? No, my legs hurt constantly. But, I also know that if I wait until later in the day to workout, life will get in the way and a thousand excuses will hijack my plans. I could pick another workout routine, but running allows for easy progress monitoring and limited excuses relating to costs, weather, and availability.

I shower, eat breakfast, and arrive at my building by 5:45am each day. I turn on my computer, turn on the lights throughout my building, pray at the flagpole, and attempt to greet each staff member as they arrive. This is only possible because each afternoon I wrap up my day by planning with an intentional focus on the start of the next day. When I arrive in the morning, I do not check my email until after the Morning Huddle, knowing that doing so will leave me with dozens of tasks that will be presented as urgent and requiring immediate attention. I work to make my priority each morning my staff. I want them to feel valued and for each huddle to be relevant to their needs and who they are as people.

If I expect my teachers to plan ahead, to be in the moment, and to focus on the learners, then that is exactly what I must model.

Sure, I have had off days. I have had days where I have hit the snooze button, where I may have overslept, or where I came in a little later and less than planned and prepared, but I can also guarantee that each time this has happened, I have spent the rest of the day playing catch up. Each time I try to steal a few extra minutes of sleep, I spend hours trying to make up for it. If I skip a morning run, I spend the afternoon feeling even more sluggish than I otherwise would. If I spend my morning putting the final touches on the day's plans instead of greeting teachers, then my focus for the day tends to be on the work and not where it should be, on the people. As a leader of my school, I recognize that this same struggle often exists with my teachers as well. Providing them with a focused process to begin each day, is possibly the best leadership strategy I have ever developed. Huddles became our game changer, not just because of what was shared each morning, but because of everything else that is impacted as a result of this intentional time together.

Huddle Up

If you get the chance to watch a football game this fall, take a look at what takes place in the huddle before each offensive play. Here is what you will see. The quarterback, the leader of the offense, will often look to the sidelines where those in charge of the game plan are standing. Using their analysis of what plays have worked in the past, and their goals for the future, the coaches will signal the next play, a play that they expect to work, that they expect will result in success, even though the reality is not every play results in a touchdown. Some are complete busts resulting in turnovers or sacks, some bring about relatively short gains, while some do send the team running down the field towards the goal. Because each player is often focused on his unique position and responsibilities, he may not see the full picture. Having a coach call in a play that allows for each player to do his part to attempt to bring about team success is where a huddle begins.

In the huddle, the quarterback is responsible for articulating the plays to each player. Bringing all of the players together, looking them in the eyes, and sending them off with a clearly articulated plan is necessary. In many huddles, as the play is outlined, one or two players may break out early to get into position, while others may linger a moment longer to gain clarity. Huddles slow down the action, put everyone in a position to succeed, bring the game plan back into focus, and help the team move forward by analyzing past performance. All of this is needed in schools today.

Here is how my huddles work. My personal cell phone is set with a number of alarms. I have an alarm telling me when to wake up, when to run, when to greet teachers, and when to start and stop my huddles. Having a "play clock" for these daily meetings is extremely important. A ten minute meeting (huddle) every single day may seem like a lot of time for communication, but if not used wisely, this can turn into a time wasting activity. I do not take attendance. I do not pass out papers. I do not do any managerial tasks during these ten minutes. Instead, at exactly 6:30am, I begin playing a playlist filled with upbeat music that is broadcast through the sound system of our cafeteria (Michael Jackson, Bobby McFerrin, etc...). When my alarm goes off ten minutes later at exactly 6:40, I greet my staff with an excited, "Good morning, everyone." If I start late, staff will show up late. If we do not jump right into the heart of the learning, value is lost and everyone will find other ways to fill the time. In a football game, the quarterback can't wait for a lineman to walk back to the line of scrimmage at his own pace. He has to be ready to lead the huddle as soon as the play is called and expects the other ten men on his team to be ready when he is.

The ten minutes of our Morning Huddle was split into four distinct sections. As a group, we spent the first two minutes celebrating the success of our peers. We demanded risk- taking and had high expectations for each staff member to go big. The first two minutes of each meeting was a celebration of risks. Last summer, when scrolling through items on the Oriental Trade Company website, just looking for small trinkets and prizes, I stumbled upon a game-changing purchase. As a school filled with pirate teachers (Thank you Dave Burgess and Quinn

Rollins) we took pride in ourselves for looking for hidden treasures and our willingness to take a chance in our pursuit of greatness. While on the OTC website I found items we now refer to as brag tags. In essence, these are dog tags with a variety of pirate symbols emblazoned onto each tag. I purchased 200 of them thinking my staff would be able to honor each other at morning meetings by bestowing tags to each other as they recognized risk-taking and tried to honor it.

What happened far surpassed my expectations. Staff honored each other and, as a result, inspired each other. Much like innovation occurring in the 1990s in Silicon Valley where tech moguls worked to enhance and build on the ideas of others at an exponential rate, staff members heard the ideas of others and not only stole them for themselves but worked to make them better. By allowing staff members to wear their brag tags daily along with their staff ID badges, students were able to see staff who were being honored for being innovative and often would ask their teacher how they earned it. The ensuing conversation then encouraged student risk-taking by modeling and celebrating at the teacher end. I am proud to say in year one we ran out of the initial two hundred brag tags ordered by the end of the first semester. Not only were staff eager to celebrate each other, but they were actively searching for risk-taking among their peers, opening their doors to others to celebrate what was happening in their rooms, and they began showing up on time each morning to see if they were being honored or to honor their peers.

On the rare occasion that there was no celebration being called for by any of the seventy-five staff members in attendance, I was sure to have one or two successes to highlight in my back pocket ready to honor those that I observed. I was careful not to share this everyday as that would create a new expectation. There is real value in having staff find value in each other, recognizing greatness in each other, and not just doing a dog and pony show for the boss in an attempt to earn a 25 cent trinket. If I found people to celebrate every day, people would simply wait for me to pay the tribute. The value came from teachers not only validating each other, but in searching for reasons to validate each other.

The next four minutes of each huddle, no more than that, were utilized for a brief professional development moment. We covered standardized grading, classroom management, parent communication, etc... Keeping our time to four minutes served so many purposes. Much like the children they educate, teachers have extremely short attention spans. Keeping things short and focused allowed for more fruit to develop than dragging out PD into a two hour after school meeting. As a professional public speaker, keeping things to four minutes is also extremely valuable to me. It forces me to focus on the focus, to pay attention to the key points and not drag things out to hear myself speak. If I am able to take large concepts and synthesize them down into bite-sized nuggets then I force myself to really know the material being presented as well.

I am not going to lie, four minutes was a tight time constraint, but it was doable. If I planned to model a pedagogical strategy, being able to fit it into a tight timeline required me to really reflect, brainstorm, and solicit the input of others. If a professional football team can get eleven men to gather into a circle, have each understand their unique responsibility, get back to the line, and hike a ball in under forty seconds, I should be able to get a group of professional educators together for four minutes and give them enough knowledge to enhance their performance.

The next two minutes of the huddle were an opportunity to reflect on the days prior. When I first began huddles, reflections were how each meeting began. I thought it was essential to begin each meeting by reviewing where we were and to analyze successes and failures from the day before. After about two weeks of this, I decided to change course. The reason was simple. This became all we did for each meeting. We never moved forward. Schools are notorious for living in the past. Reflection is critical, but reflection is not the same thing as reminiscing, complaining, or telling stories. Reflection helps us grow if we are able to take a critical look at where we are and either celebrate or improve. Bringing reflection to the last half of our huddles allowed us to make connections from where we were to what we had just learned. This was a key step to moving forward.

Sometimes the reflection was simply a recap of an evolved practice. Sometimes it was an online survey where staff got to share where they were and where they needed to go. We used a variety of protocols, each with their own pros and cons. None took more than two minutes, however, because the last two minutes were the most critical of the entire meeting.

Each huddle adjourned with a challenge. Just as Tom Brady and Russell Wilson inspire their teams with a hand clap, a chant of their team names, or simple high fives, the huddle inspired action. After a huddle, football teams then step to the line, hike the ball, and implement what was just discussed. The coaches watch, analyze, and then plan the next steps depending on the results. Having a huddle just to huddle is a waste of time. The final two minutes of each Morning Huddle at my school was where we discussed the day's "look fors". It was where we stated what staff members should be prepared to do to achieve success and what we would be reflecting on in the future. We provided challenges to teachers to make them step out of their comfort zones and try something new. Often the challenges were related to our four minutes of professional learning, but sometimes they were designed just to keep the pedagogical sword sharp. Below is a brief list of some of the challenges teachers were presented with:

- Provide 50 hugs to 50 different kids
- Use no paper
- Do not use anything that has to be plugged in
- Take your class outside of your classroom
- Celebrate success all day and provide no negative reinforcement,
- Switch rooms with a peer
- Wear a costume
- Use Play Doh or Lego to teach the concepts

With each new learning, we were inspired to try something new. What we discovered was that no challenge was the silver bullet or magic pill, but each inspired us to stretch and grow by taking us out of our comfort zone and making us expand our instructional repertoire. Like an athlete who goes for a run daily in order to try and build strength and speed learns, he has to work in some cross training, some hills, and speed workouts, to improve. He can plod along, putting in the miles every day, on the same track, but eventually he will plateau. In order to keep getting better, he has to change things up every once in a while. The same is true with us as teachers. We can stick to our routines and be comfortable, but if we want to really see greatness and constant improvement, we need to add a little variety to stretch our abilities and become the strongest teachers we can.

 "Grace is helping others know you will always pick them up when they fall down. Pride is acting like you never fall."

In the beginning
Emily Leach

Teacher, Michigan, @emiliyleach14

Early in my teaching career, I received my yearly evaluation for the first time from the assistant principal. The evaluation was based on a single class period observation using a rubric that was unknown to me. The class she observed was an engineering elective that was new to both me and the school. For my lesson, I had designed a WebQuest for the students to do in groups on the principles of engineering while I pulled groups into the hall to test the racers they had created using the engineering design method. I was proud of my choice of activities to display for my observation. I had students up and moving, doing hands- on learning, and working in groups. The lesson also showed off my tech-savvy skills and ability to have multiple things going on in my classroom at once. I thought that all this was pretty impressive for a new teacher. I really put myself out there to do a nontraditional lesson, , and was certain it would pay off.

I was wrong.

A few weeks later I received my official evaluation write-up. I was given the rating of, 'minimally effective'. Among the list of areas I could improve were: the students were talking too much, I needed a longer tape measurer for testing the racers, and my classroom management was poor.

Needless to say, I was devastated. I defended my lesson by explaining that the students were working in groups so, of course, they would be talking and that I didn't know that we had a longer tape measurer in the school (I wasn't aware of the ones used in track and field). As for the poor classroom management piece, I was given an audio version of the Harry Wong classic, "First Days of School", to listen to.

As a result of this entire experience, I was never able to accept any sort of feedback from this administrator for the rest of the time she was in the building. My trust in her was irreparably damaged. As a new teacher, I had been in an extremely vulnerable position. It took me a long time to recover from the experience.

Looking back, I realize that I did learn something about teaching from the whole debacle. I am always encouraging my students to take risks with their learning, and I would never want them to have the same feelings toward me that I did toward my administrator. As a result, I do my best to treat my students with respect, individuality, and sensitivity. Feedback is critical to growth, but before it can be received trust has to be earned.

BOLD NEXT STEPS

1. Identify a meeting or a committee that is in existence simply because it has always been there and eliminate it, TODAY. You do not need to offer an explanation, just announce that it is done.

2. Find a way to celebrate risk-taking. Don't blow smoke and set the stage that everyone needs an award. Watering it down will bring about watered down results. State that everyone can achieve success but then set the bar high and celebrate any time someone attempts to reach it, even if they fail miserably.

3. Challenge yourself. Publicly state a BIG goal that you have that will stretch you. If you can't think of one, solicit feedback from others, then share your successes and more importantly your struggles as you relentlessly pursue success.

BOLD REFLECTIONS

CHAPTER FIVE

HIRE THE BEST, CHALLENGE THE BEST, CHEER ON THE BEST

THE EDUCATIONAL LANDSCAPE has changed so much in recent years, it is almost unrecognizable to many of us when we compare it to the schools we attended as children. But this is a good thing, because the world we live in has evolved as well. Gone are the days of TV dinners, rotary phones, and gas guzzling station wagons. We now live in a world of innovation and constant change. A world where there literally is an app for everything. A world that rewards creativity. A world unlike anything any of us could have imagined when we sat behind our desks as kids and stared at our teachers while daydreaming about the world of tomorrow.

The primary purpose of formalized schooling is to equip our current students with the skills and abilities to succeed independent of school, to thrive on their own and to have the ability and capacity to evolve with the world around them, or perhaps better stated, to lead the next evolution of the world. Our responsibility is not to longingly look back on the educational experience we came from and work our hardest to replicate it today. Our duty is to look to the future and try to equip our students with the skills necessary to adapt to whatever is thrown at them.

Our students today, deserve teachers who understand that school is different. The world is different. Children are different. And as a result, their classrooms must be different.

As a school leader, the most important part of my job is hiring teachers. Teachers are the ones who will be working with students day in and day out. They are the influencers, the life shapers, the destiny makers. As much as I want to believe a great administrator is what makes a great school, the reality is, it is a great teacher who can help shape a great life. My job is to hire, support, cheer, and get out of the way. If I hire well, the rest is easy. So how do I make sure that only the best are in front of our kids? Is this even possible when there is a nationwide teacher shortage, when the average teacher only lasts 3.3 years in a classroom, when so many teachers have to work two jobs just to stay out of poverty? Can this be done? The answer is empathically, YES!

I could sit around and complain about the impossibility of the task. I could yell at state and local politicians to do something about the broken system, or I can embrace the fact that all great change in America begins at the grassroots level, and embark on a quest to find those who want to fight the fight with me. If the US Marine Corps can encourage The Few, The Proud, and The Brave, to take up arms and defend our country in foreign lands, surely I can find a few amazing individuals each year who are willing to take on the challenge to change a generation. And that, my friends, is exactly what I have been able to do.

Teaching, we've been told for years, is both an art and a science. Teaching is not a profession that requires a passion for assigning work and reading. Teaching is not a profession that can be replaced by curriculum and textbooks. Teaching is a profession that requires a passion for people and a desire for progress. It is not a profession seeking perfection and compliance. Teaching is a profession that requires risk-taking and reflection.

When I am selecting teachers, I care less about their content knowledge, and more about their ability to engage and inspire. I care less about their high school G.P.A. and more about the diversity of their social media followers. I care less about the last book they read and more about the shows scheduled to be recorded on their home DVR. I want teachers who are living life, who have a passion for today, and a desire to change tomorrow. Sure, I want people who know their content and can address the standards, but getting someone who simply knows the difference between an antecedent and a pronoun is no match for someone who knows how to get students excited about that difference. I am looking to hire people who can inspire people, not just a teacher who can present content to students.

Who You Were Does Not Define Who You Will Be

Recently at my school we did an activity that required staff members to bring in a picture of themselves from middle school to display along with the following message, "It's not about who you were, it's who you are that determines who you will be." This activity helped us show our students who we were as children and give them hope for their future. Beyond that, it allowed each of us a chance to take a trip down memory lane by flipping through old photo albums. While I was flipping through one of mine, I stumbled upon a picture I had long ago forgotten about. It was an image of me as a twelve year old boy sitting in a large cardboard box.

I grew up as a Navy brat. Having a father who served in the military meant that my family was asked to relocate often. As a matter of fact, I attended sixteen different schools growing up. While we were relocating, so were all of our household goods. I spent a great deal of my childhood packing and unpacking. The image displayed in this forgotten about photograph showed a picture of me soon after making one of our many moves. My family had just moved into a new house and all of my toys and clothes had just been delivered. Looking back on it now, I remember that I had been asked to spend a month surviving with only the items that could fit into one suitcase. On the day this picture was taken, all of my other personal possessions had arrived. All of my toys, clothes, sports equipment, everything. When my parents came in to my room to take this picture with what I assume was a recently unpacked camera they assumed I would be playing in a huge pile of toys, instead they found a pile of my toys sitting on the floor next to me and me seated inside a large box, with a hat on my head turned backward, and sunglasses on. I had turned one of our packing boxes into a fighter jet and I was the pilot. What the picture did not show was that the next day that same box was converted into a racecar, the day after that it was King Tut's tomb. That box sparked hours of creative fun. Was that what the designers of that box intended? No way. It was designed to hold personal items for easy shipping. My parents had even taken a permanent marker to the side of it and labeled it Dave's Toys. I had taken my imagination and turned it into so much more.

This is what our students need to be able to do more often. As educators, we read articles, explore Twitter, read books like this one, and attend conferences in an attempt to hear the latest trick necessary to increase our bottom line (student achievement). Unfortunately, what we often do as a result of all of this "learning" is place ourselves in a box, slap a label on it, and lose our creativity. We think one initiative, one tool, one pre-packaged/pre-labeled program is going to be the answer. We try to find a script to follow; we forget we have kids to reach and get frustrated when we don't get the intended results.

For the past ten years, the terms formative and summative assessment have been used by countless "experts" to describe how we need to evaluate student learning. Often teachers learn about these two formats and try to craft two different types of assessments to fit their varied needs. We are told that teachers must create formative assessments in order to evaluate their own teacher effectiveness. We are told teachers must create summative assessments in order to evaluate student learning. We place these assessments into two separate boxes, label them, and use them only for their pre-planned designated purposes of either evaluating ourselves or students. Don't get me wrong. Using formative and summative assessments are a crucial component of high-quality teaching. At my own schools we have spent the decade talking about little else, but what we lose sight of is the fact that the best assessments serve both purposes, for both the teacher and the students, not one exclusively. Placing a label on an assessment prior to using the assessment is unnecessarily restricting. Teachers should be able to give an assessment and use it formatively and summatively. The label on the assessment should not be applied until after it has been used. Placing it on prematurely places us in a labeled box. If we label it summative and we do not get the intended results indicating student learning, does this mean a teacher should not adjust his or her instruction? If we label it formative but every kid shows mastery, are we not supposed to claim this as evidence of proficiency? A great assessment allows us to use it formatively to evaluate our own instruction AND summatively by assessing student understanding. It is how the task is used, not how it is designed, that yields results.

Assessment is critical. Teachers must be diligent to determine the validity and reliability of an assessment, but that does not mean they must limit themselves to the label. When working on classroom instruction, teachers must not fool themselves into thinking there is only one way for a child to learn. There are countless ways for students to learn, just as there are countless ways for students to show what they have learned. We need to avoid putting our students into boxes that are already labeled. We need to avoid telling students there is only one way to do anything. We need to know how the story of our classroom will unfold, but we may not necessarily know the themes that will emerge. If you are a leader with evaluation and supervision responsibilities, you have to remember that evaluations are assessments and how you treat them is how your followers will treat them. If you evaluate to judge, define, and label, that is exactly how your staff will use assessment. If you use observations as a mechanism for personal reflection and planning future professional development, then your staff will do the same.

Great authors understand this. Titles of books are not written before the story is complete. They wait until they have developed an entire plot, then look for a way to synthesize the message. Singers do not determine which songs will be singles or the titles of their albums until the entire record has been crafted. As teachers, we need to learn to take our labels off and just go.

I think about my oldest son who likes to play with Lego's. He has countless sets. He has bricks of every shape and color. When his sets are purchased they always come in a box with directions. He used to follow the directions, assemble the pieces just right, and then…nothing. Once he had followed the manufacturer's directions, he saw his job as done. He was not asked to be creative, inventive, or investigative. We now buy his Lego's, toss the directions in the garbage, throw the pieces into a bin with the rest of them, and say "Have fun" and it is up to him to learn, create, and "think outside of the box."

The kids we are teaching today will be asked to demonstrate that they understand the world in a way that is much different than we ever had to. Sure, they will need to be able to follow directions, but more than that, they will be asked to write directions. They will be asked to identify problems and create solutions. They will all be asked to serve as an engineer in some capacity. They will be asked to design solutions, experiment, troubleshoot, and fail repeatedly.

As teachers, don't put yourself, or your students, in a labeled box. Of course you need to stay organized, but the only time a box needs a label on it is when items are being moved from one place to another. Once it has arrived, scrub the labels off and let the creativity begin. Don't force your students to learn the way you learn. Let them learn how to learn. Don't force them to be assessed using one template. Let them demonstrate understanding by being creative. Help them identify the problems, but let them generate the solutions. Don't stick to the script when an adlib is necessary. Don't tell your students to climb out of the box because it was designed for something else. If your students climb in, help them create something that has value. I am so lucky that on that day, thirty-some years ago, my parents let my toys sit on the bedroom floor and captured a picture of me playing in an empty box. A box that allowed my creative energies to be utilized. A box that was designed for one purpose, but was repurposed into something that has lasted a lifetime. That box is a great memory. Had it only been used to pack up some old GI Joes, it would have been recycled and forgotten about. Because the label was removed, it instead has become a lasting memory. A memory that has changed the way I parent, the way I teach, and the way I lead. The past serves as a great catalyst for the future, but we cannot use it as a model for replication.

I hire those who have been inspired and hope to inspire. I hire those who can share their memories and as a result, create hope. I hire those who can look back and think of ways to make the future better. I hire those who understand that the path to being highly effective is not paved with repetition, but with reflection.

Good Day, Bad Day

For those who have ever interviewed with me, or served on an interview team with me, you can attest that there are only two questions that I consider important. Serving on interview committees we always ask 8-10 questions so that all participants are able to hear responses appropriate to their interests, but for me, they are only two that matter. They are always my first and last questions. Feel free to take note if you have a meeting coming up with me in the future.

The first question I ask is very similar to the first question asked at every interview. Everyone wants to know who you are, what your experience is, and where you went to college. I am a firm believer that, just like in the classroom we should never ask students a question that Google can answer. I should never ask a question during an interview that a resume can address. A candidate's resume is what got him or her to the interview. It is their personality and passion that will determine whether or not they get the job. So, instead of just asking the candidates to introduce themselves, I begin by introducing my school. I describe it as though it is my child. I describe its strengths and its struggles. I describe the way it looks, the way it sounds, and its latest celebrations. Remember, a school is not the brick and mortar; a school is the people inside. My goal is to provide a realistic preview of the job. I want the candidate across the table to know from our very first interaction that this school is my pride and joy. Every child in my school is someone else's baby and I take that very seriously. It is my responsibility to remind the people I work with daily that we are not just chasing scores, we are changing destinies. As I spend five minutes describing the wonder and passion that exists within the walls of my school, I then ask very simply, "So tell us how your past has equipped you to work with us in changing lives."

By front loading who we are and describing our strengths, weaknesses, and passions, I am able to draw more from the candidates.

They hear me say the word "us". They know we are about changing lives. They know that simply telling me what their major in college was, is not going to cut it. The first question is like a first date. It helps me determine whether or not I want to take the relationship further. It is a chance to let both sides figure out if there is any potential or whether or not we should just cut our losses early on.

The final question I ask candidates, if they make it that far, is always the hardest question for candidates to answer. I have had many seasoned teachers sitting on committees with me, saying, "I am so glad I already have this job, because I wouldn't be able to answer that." And you know what, those teachers then know what my expectations are. The question is a simple one, but the answers given say so much. Take a look at it and then see if you can answer it. Are you ready? I promise you the build-up is over the top for the simplicity you are about to read. The question is:

"At the end of the day, how do you know if it has been a good day or a bad day?"

That's it. Seems simple enough, right? Not so fast.

Throughout the years I have heard, literally, hundreds of answers to this question. It is a question with no right answer, but countless wrong answers. This question is designed to assess reflection, optimism, and outlook. For many of us, when we end our day, we look back on defining moments. We resonate on the one child who got under our skin. The one child who didn't get it. The one parent who hung up on us. The one staff member who passed by without acknowledgement. For others, the day is always sunshine and rainbows, while for others, there is always a dark cloud. Some live in the moment espousing that there is always tomorrow, while others hold on to yesterday with a vendetta to make amends. The question with no answer is not designed to stump anyone. It is designed to emphasize the importance of reflection.

Each day we must begin our day with a purpose. Our purpose cannot be to simply cross tasks off of our list. Our purpose has to be to make a measurable difference. Throughout the day, the decisions we make either get us closer to success or closer to failure. Circumstances will pop up. Life will get in the way. Others will try to exert an influence, but we own our progress.

When I meet a candidate for the first time, I am looking for someone who recognizes this. I am looking for goal setters and dreamers. I am looking for doers and action planners. I want people willing to step up and own their impact. Teachers must know that they make a difference and be willing to own that, both when things are going well and when they go adrift. Teachers must know the difference between success for EACH student and success for EVERY student. Teachers must measure their own success, not by their tenacity and desire, but by the students they teach. Teachers must own that it is their job to make students smile, passionate, curious, and informed. Teachers must be able to measure their success and ability to do each of these and must know that many days they will fail in one or more areas with one or more students, but this does not make them a failure. Highly effective, does not mean perfect. It means vulnerable, open, honest, and progressive. It means a willingness to create it, own it, and fix it, whatever "it" is. If you want to be a teacher for me, you must be willing to embrace Bold Humility, yourself. Your ability to know what is working and what is not, is what "it" is all about.

So what do you do if you have a candidate with all of the passion in the world, a smile that is contagious, and an infectious love for learning who also lacks experience, struggles with identifying Best Practices with pedagogy, and only a basic knowledge of content? Well, assuming no other candidates possess all of these attributes in high quantities, you hire them, and you coach them. Pedagogy and content can be taught. Passion and love cannot. Just as teachers must fully embrace their power to change the lives of their students, quality administrators must believe they have the power to shape and cultivate teachers. We have to stop the search for the teaching candidates who will give us the quickest short-term results and begin to embrace the search for the person who will have the most fruitful career. Give me a teacher willing to make a difference for thirty years over the teacher who will rock it for the next three years, any day of the week. To use a sports analogy, I would rather draft a quality prospect who will grow up in the system, than acquire a rental player in free agency who I know will get us a trophy one year and leave us re-building again the following year. In changing destinies, we need to be creating dynasties and legacies.

The idea of a leader being a coach is a struggle in today's educational world so filled with accountability. To be an effective coach, you must acquire trust. Trust requires vulnerability. Vulnerability requires a willingness to not just show strengths, but to be truly humble and share struggles as well. All across America today, teachers are feeling beat up. They are tied to data. They are observed for effectiveness. They receive generalized labels as a result of the evidence collected. In many states, merit pay has come into the equation. Teachers are compensated based on their final evaluation ratings, causing many to shy away from ever sharing a vulnerability in fear that it may impact the money they can bring home to their families. And we wonder why innovation is disappearing from our schools. We have driven it out. I am all for accountability. I believe teachers should be evaluated based on student outcomes, but what I am not in favor of, is when we tell teachers exactly what to do and use compliance as our guide, not creativity, flexibility, and differentiation.

Here is the dilemma we face. We have kids who need us today. We have kids who show up for school every single day who need the absolute best from every adult in their lives. The accountability mandates in place across America recognize this and attempt to put pressure on schools to ensure that only the best are available for our kids. That makes perfect sense, but here is what often happens. Schools hire new teachers, teachers with a developing skill set, and are expected to measure their performance using the same criteria as those of veteran staff members with more instructional tools in their toolbox, developed from experience. These new teachers are then compared to their peers, and are then, often times left feeling defeated at the end of the school year and within a few short years, before being given the opportunity to become an expert, decide that teaching just isn't for them. Schools then repeat the pattern over and over again in a quest to find the diamond in the rough. So instead of taking a few years to groom teachers into career educators, schools are left every year plugging holes left by teachers who left the career feeling unsupported, unwanted, and undervalued. The solution, again, could be the one where we sit around and complain about the brokenness of the system, or we can play within the confines of the box and make it better.

I am happy to say, the teachers I have been able to hire truly are the best of the best. I have already described how I find them, but the real magic is how we keep them.

Triangles are Stronger Than Circles

In leadership training, we often learn about our inner circles. These are described as trusted advisors, those who are given access to privileged information, and can help guide decision making. In some schools, these inner circles have titles such as Leadership Teams, School Improvement Teams, Data Teams, etc. You know what I am referring to. To those within the inner circle, those well within the circle, typically the principal and assistants, these teams are seen as critical to school success. What they fail to take notice of is the constant dance, negotiation, and debate that is occurring among those on the fringe or just outside the circle. You see, a circle has no defined sides. It has no edges or corners. It has an infinite number of entry points. When we have inner circles, often times we create a sense of competition as people attempt to work their way inside. Sometimes this is done by pushing. Sometimes it's done by pulling. Sometimes it is done by just squeezing into a space already occupied and trying to make room. Inner circles may be great for decision making, but they are climate and culture destroyers.

Everyone in a school knows who is a part of the "in crowd". Everyone knows that inner circles are actually concentric circles, like a target with a bull's eye in the middle, with some standing close to the center and others a little further to the edge. It is the edge that causes the struggle. The center is where the most value exists, with fewer points awarded the more you move away. The same is true with this leadership approach. An inner circle creates a multi-layered hierarchy of competition, debate, and strife that so often is unnecessary. In an attempt to create trust and transparency, I use a leadership triangle approach, as opposed to a circle.

The major difference in this approach is that my triangle has three defined sides. I make it known that any time I am working to make a big decision I will work to hear from two other sources, other than mine. What I typically do is identify two individuals who have established rapport and respect with their peers, are willing to be vocal and honest, yet also willing to engage and debate. I announce who these individuals are, to allow for a period of conversation and research, then sit down with just the three of us and hash it out. The people with an active role in the triangle vary based on the decision being made. I work to diversify and actually keep a spreadsheet of names on my computer to remember who I have utilized. Different problems have different triangles. Using the same person over and over again is no better than having a circle. Everyone knows this person is in the bull's eye and becomes a target for jealousy. Triangles really are amazing. The three branches of government we have in America operate as a triangle approach to leadership. Triangles are shapes of strength in architecture, often used to hold up bridges and roadways. They also work to make teachers better.

As the designated school leader, I understand that I am often susceptible to hearing "yes speak" when in a decision-making mode. To my face, everyone agrees with me. Behind closed doors or in a staff lounge, real feelings can get shared. This happens in every school building in America, but my goal is to try and limit this. I want real feedback. I want real dialogue. I want conversation and collaboration. The triangle encourages this as I am always outnumbered by others. Entering a decision-making process with two other people, each of us has the opportunity to create an ally and to persuade the majority. I understand that some believe the final decision making should always fall on a building principal, the designated leader, for hiring, for staffing, for school improvement, etc. but I am a believer that my role is not to make every decision but instead it is to drive the process and support the decisions that are made. It is a leader's job to put the right people in the room, not to script the decisions that come out of the room.

The school is not my school. It is, and needs to be, a reflection of every person who walks the halls. Just as the role of a parent is not to create perfect children, but to raise future empowered adults, my job as the principal is not to create dependent staff members incapable of making decisions without me, but to create a collection of individuals who thrive on discourse, debate, and problem solving. My goal is to have a collection of individuals who do not approach me and ask for solutions to their problems, but instead seek my input on how they can best solve their own problems. The difference is huge.

I recognize in my building, I am not the "go to" person for everyone, nor can I be. Not only is it an impossible task for me to give everyone the attention they need and deserve, but I do not have the knowledge and experience to guide everyone to greatness. As the boss, many teachers want to assume that I have all of the answers. Many principals want their teachers to feel like they do have all of the answers, but I am well aware of my weaknesses. Trying to fake my way through expert status simply makes me look like a fraud and destroys trust. I know this first-hand. It is why I now believe leaders should spend more time trying to communicate and less time trying to be competent.

Instead, using my triangulation of leadership, I align support with everyone both personally and professionally. Triangles allow for relationships to form that do not often form in large committees and subcommittees allowing me to get a better pulse on where individuals stand, what they need, and what they believe. My role is to not just create good policies and procedures, but to also keep a pulse on how I can support and coach each individual I work with. The conversations that often develop from triangle dialogue is better than anything else I have stumbled upon.

Coaching is very rarely done best by those who were the best. Basketball fans can tell you how coaching worked out for Michael Jordan. It didn't. It was also a disaster for my childhood idol, Isaiah Thomas. It is often the second-tier talent that makes the best guide later on. The problem is, often those who excel in their craft have a difficult time understanding why others can't do likewise. They feel like if they were great, everyone can be great. Their lens of expectations can then become skewed and frustrations bubble up instead of opportunities. What tends to make for a great coach is also what makes a great person. A coach must be a manager of personalities. A coach must be relatable, optimistic, hopeful, and encouraging. It's why oftentimes in schools, successful athletic coaches are also popular people. An instructional coach should have the same level of popularity. If an athletic coach can be popular among students an instructional coach should be popular among peers.

In each school I have been in, I have hired instructional coaches, regularly placed them in decision making triangles, and made my selection process for who fills these roles not because of inherent content knowledge, but instead because of their personality and persuasive abilities. I have no shame admitting, the academic success seen at the schools I have been lucky enough to work at has nothing to do with me, other than my decision to hire these amazing people. When you are able to get people, amazing people, hire them. You can always train content and pedagogy, but you cannot always inspire passion and commitment to grow and improve.

 "You can have growth or you can have compliance. You cannot have both."

WITH A LITTLE HELP FROM MY FRIENDS
LIZ RIBAUDO

Teacher, Florida, @LizRibaudo

Teaching is a profession unlike any other. It can be one of the most rewarding professions, but it can also be one of the loneliest and most isolating professions. When preparing for this profession, future teachers receive more tips, tricks, and advice than most know what to do with! The one thing that no one prepares you for is how isolating teaching can be if you do not have the support that you need and a strong team surrounding you.

Now don't get me wrong. I absolutely love teaching with every ounce of my being, and I know that this is where I am supposed to be. But, that doesn't mean that some days aren't rough. You might feel like a complete failure (for a variety of reasons) on more than one occasion. You might question if you can really change the lives of your students. You may even question if you can keep pushing through all of the state mandates and keep your eyes focused on what truly matters, the kids.

This is where having your team, or your tribe, comes in. Your tribe will be your biggest cheerleaders through your new (and sometimes crazy-sounding) ideas for your classroom. They will help you learn from your mistakes and grow into the teacher that you want to become, the teacher you were meant to be. Your tribe will also lift you up on days you're not sure you can keep going. They will remind you of why you chose to become a teacher. They will help you not feel alone.

If you're lucky, you will have the support and guidance of

some amazing teachers, coaches, and administrators at your school. Bring these people into your tribe. If you are not so lucky in this way, don't stop looking! Your tribe is out there. You were not meant to be alone in this profession.

When looking for your tribe, please understand your tribe doesn't have to be other teachers on your grade level. It doesn't even have to be other teachers at your school. It may include some teachers and staff from your school, as well as schools across the country. With the guidance and encouragement of my principal, I turned to Twitter to help me find other like-minded teachers to help keep me encouraged, learn from, and grow with. Whoever they are, and wherever they are, find them, love them, and support them and know that they will love and support you in the same way.

BOLD NEXT STEPS

1. Find a picture of yourself from when you were in school, the more embarrassing the better. Display it in your classroom or office and use it to tell your story. Remind your students or staff what your dreams and hopes were when you were in school.

2. Expand your tribe. If you are not actively engaged in social media, start now. The individuals who have provided testimonials in this book are part of my tribe. Follow them and expand your people power.

3. Identify two people, only two people, who can help you make your next big decision. It's OK to start small by trying to decide where to go get lunch, but work towards finding those trusted members of your triangle who can keep you aligned on your priorities with what matters most.

BOLD REFLECTIONS

_____

_____

_____

_____

_____

_____

_____

_____

_____

_____

_____

_____

_____

_____

_____

_____

_____

_____

_____

_____

_____

_____

_____

CHAPTER SIX

CHALLENGING THE STATUS QUO IS A MINDFIELD

LET ME STATE, again, I am not a perfect administrator. Not even close. As a person I have flaws. As a school leader, I have made countless mistakes. It's been said before by others, "A leader who admits his mistakes is not revealing any new information to those around him, only to himself." Those I aim to serve know my shortcomings. As a leader, I have people who despise my style. As an educator, I have stakeholders who do not see the world the same way I do. As a man, I disappoint and let down those I love, but all of this is also what makes me human.

As I write this, I am in my nineteenth year as a professional educator and am working in my sixth school. Most of my job transitions have been my choice, but not all of them. It is important to remember that all practices, policies, procedures, and beliefs espoused by others are based on someone's perspective of reality. Each school I have worked in has had a different way to do business. No two buildings, no two districts seem to do anything the same way. But, that is OK. Being a leader means we assume the good and doubt the bad. We cannot enter any situation or any environment and assume that past practices that we may disagree with today were developed with negative intentions yesterday. We must believe that everyone acts from a place of good, yet we are called upon to make things better. Real leaders spend their time connecting, not correcting.

It is a slippery and potentially dangerous place to be when you feel the need to change the way things are done, especially when those who may have created the structures you are trying to change are still employed in, around, or above you in your system's hierarchy. Determining when to challenge **What Is** to explore **What Could Be** is perhaps one of the most important leadership lessons to learn. You cannot fight every battle. You cannot challenge every idea. You cannot push back against every MINDset. Decision making in leadership can really be a MINDfield and it is up to you to determine which MINDS to challenge and which you should avoid.

It is essential to remember that you are where you are to try and make the lives of children better and you can only do that if you are able to stay where you are. Every new leader steps into his or her new role with visions of a renaissance. These visions are similar to the dreams a new teacher has of changing the world through every student taught. This is a noble passion, but one that can quickly become defeating and deflating. There's a reason so many teachers, and so many administrators, leave their careers after only a couple of years. The impact that consistent staff turnover has on a school, and each child it serves, is monumental. Momentum is a key component of learning and each time it is disrupted by staff change there is a period of startup required. We have to be strategic in determining what to change and when. Not every hill is worth dying on.

A Focused Leader Says "No" to Good Ideas All of the Time

Think about a child learning to ride his bike. Each time the new rider has to start riding again, after an interruption, there is the need to line the pedals up just right. There may be a pep talk required if the interruption was a result of falling down. There may be a realignment of the wheels to point them forward, and then there may be a need for a big push before balance is regained and forward progress can resume. The same is true in a school when leaders have to start over again when trying to gain movement towards greater success and milestones. Each time there is a break in the action, just trying to get things lined back up again requires effort. Keep the momentum going by getting the work done, while also keeping yourself on the job and not on the job hunt. You can't lead if you're not around. Pick and choose your battles wisely.

It is so important to maintain focus on your "why", the reason you do what you do, the forest in the midst of the trees. It is so easy to find yourself distracted by smoke screens, by fluff, by influences beyond your control. It is easy to step in and believe it is your job to fix everything, to enhance everything, to reinvent wheels, and fight every battle, but that couldn't be further from the truth.

When I first became a parent, I was told that as a dad I should say "Yes" as often as possible. That way when I had to say "No" it would be heard and not misunderstood. That parenting advice is also great leadership advice. You cannot fight every fight. When too many fights are being fought, you run the risk of being blindsided.

America is a world superpower. As a nation, we have tremendous influence over the world, but we cannot, and should not, get involved in every debate and conflict raging around the planet. Some issues have a direct influence on us and need a direct response. Some have a more indirect influence on our livelihood and may require a more subtle approach, whereas others, really don't have an impact on us at all and will only serve as a distraction to what really matters to us if we get involved. As a leader, you must decide early on what battles are worth the fight and what can wait. Good leaders say "yes" as often as possible. Focused leaders say "no" to good ideas all the time. The trick is to identify what is really important and what can wait.

Do you want to increase parental involvement at your school, but want to also decrease the number of parents walking their kids to the classrooms at the start of the school day? Which matters more? Do you hate homework, but think student engagement is the key to quality feedback and learning? Which requires your attention first. Is bullying an issue at your school, but a limited-electives schedule available for students has become a hot topic among the parents? Which issue matters more. There are literally thousands of topics that can become hot button items if we let them.

As a leader, your staff is not only influenced by the opinion you publicly share, but also by the disagreements you give your time to. Time is your most valuable asset and by simply providing others with some of your time you run the risk of becoming distracted you from your primary purpose. You give credibility to a battle that may not be worth fighting. Just like American diplomats serving in other countries around the world are asked to not only carry forth the agenda of the president, but they also get to help sift through the issues brought forth by others to determine whether issues belong on the president's desk or not. This isn't to say that not everyone deserves a voice. It's just that not every issue can be dealt with right away. Not everything has the same weight or importance and not everything carries with it the same political capital.

I understand the Butterfly Effect, the belief that even the flapping wings of a tiny insect where you are can impact the weather on the other side of the world. As an administrator, it is important to see the long term impacts of our decisions, but more importantly we need to remember the long term goals we have for our students.

On my desk in my office, I have an old beat up blue three ring binder. I call it Honolulu Blue (My other Detroit Lions fans will understand the root of this name). This binder serves as my Leadership Bible, or maybe more accurately, my Leadership Atlas. Much like the glove box of a car in the 1980s, this binder contains the roadmaps for where I hope to go with my school and district in the future. Helping me move away from simply navigating the proverbial road blocks of today, the binder allows me to always stay future focused and engaged in the process of moving forward.

Evolving each year, old Honolulu Blue gets an edit each summer. I have divided him (yes, he is male even though I know men never look at maps) into five chapters, one chapter for each of the next five years. As one year comes to an end, I reflect on progress made, make adjustments to future years, and add a new fifth year to the end. Honolulu Blue contains School Improvement Goals, Academic Improvement Goals,

Staff Capacity Goals, as well as the anticipated strategies for obtaining success with each goal. The binder is not a paper and pencil copy of my building School Improvement Plan. It is not a list of programs, curriculum, and quick fix solutions. It is a plan and a purpose that tries to ensure that all that is done is connected, integrated, and aligned so that I am not caught chasing the next best thing and falling guilty of creating programming built on gimmicks instead of aligned around people.

People are what drive the need for the binder. The names of people line the pages. The chapter for next year contains more than 150 pages. There is a page for each staff member I work with along with notes identifying their passions, skills, and fears. I identify the students each staff member is charged with developing deeper bonds with. I list training needs and opportunities for each adult, and I identify the day I will be calling each co-worker on the phone to remind him/her why they took this job and why he/she is so valuable to our team. I have a page that I call the Web of Influence. It is basically a list of teacher's names spread out around the page with lines connecting those who have solid personal connections. This web helps me as I develop my triangles for decision making and as I create the master schedule each summer. Each page also identifies the unique responsibility each team member will play in helping us meet our collective goals. The bottom line is that each person plays a role. Each person is valuable to our collective success. Each person plays a part individually, yet also has an impact on others either through their influence, their relationships, or their knowledge. I expect it from my teachers and my principals because I expect it of myself.

As the leader, it is my job to identify and articulate this, just as it is the responsibility of a teacher to differentiate for the needs of each of her students. I am a firm believer that students are the reason behind all that we do. They are not only our job security, but they fill our passion and purpose. There are some adults, however, that use this belief to act recklessly all in the name of "What's best for kids." often losing sight of long-term goals and those who have the greatest impact on those same children. If we want to do what's best for kids, we have to do what's best for our teachers and staff.

Influence and pay are often connected in an inverse relationship. If you are "on the top" you must protect those at "the bottom" of the job hierarchy. Too often in organizations, we see individuals who carry with them the title "boss" and erroneously believe that this also equates to influence. Often it is the "boss" who makes the biggest miscalculation. I absolutely believe that respect is given and not earned. I wholeheartedly believe that respect is a basic human right. That is not to say that respect, authority, and power all equate to influence. Influence and the power to change thoughts, actions, and beliefs very rarely come from positional authority.

I am no fool. I completely recognize that sometimes simply because of my title in my own district, my ability to influence is negated. I have a big office. I have a private phone line. I have degrees and have written books. I get to travel the country speaking and presenting, yet as much as I love all of this, at times all of this can actually get in the way of getting the job done if I allow it to. In an attempt to change mindsets and create enhanced culture, some may rebuff my ideas and suggestions simply because I am the boss and for no other reason. One thing that I have recognized is that often in schools, influence and pay have an inverse relationship. If you are a leader and you really want to change your school, don't try to do it alone. If you want the masses to buy in, convince your secretaries, custodians, and paraprofessionals first. They are often the toughest critics, your most vocal employees, and the ones with the greatest power to leverage your leadership. The real power does not come from those with the biggest paycheck. It comes from those with the biggest audience.

We can read reports all over the internet these days that new teachers are leaving the profession in record numbers. There are teacher shortages in every state as current schools and districts search high and low for people willing to take on this rewarding, yet draining profession. New teachers enter the profession fresh out of college, filled with visions of changing destinies, instilling hope to the hopeless, and bringing about a new generation of world leaders, only to abandon their own dream, beaten by the same world they are trying to change.

With a three year old child still in my house, it is fair to say I will need to keep working for at least another twenty years. This far into my chosen career I don't have the luxury to simply pack up and try something new. Lucky for me, that won't be needed because I LOVE my job and I have learned the secret to longevity. I know not every hill is worth dying on, yet some are, and it's those hills that renew my commitment and passion. They don't dampen it. Old Honolulu Blue helps me stay focused on what is important, who to influence, and sometimes even more importantly, what fights are worth the effort.

There is No Bigger Obstacle Than an Ego

As a new teacher, two decades ago, I was ready to set the world on fire. I came to work every day relishing in what some would describe as hero worship as hundreds of 12 year olds hang on my every word in my middle school classroom. It's crazy how big my ego was able to swell simply because I was able to entertain some pre-teens who felt like I was the smartest person on earth. Because of that, I often felt invincible and felt like that same competence that I brought to the classroom for my students should be accepted just as openly by the adults I encountered daily...boy was I wrong. My own arrogance and belief in myself often caused me to live and work on an island, fighting for the principles that I held true...every single principle.

I was that guy that caused every staff meeting to run thirty minutes over time because I would challenge the new dress code policy; I would debate the grading scale; I would question the need for yet another fire drill. Nothing was ever good enough, nothing that is, unless it was the way I would do things.

Within a few years, my arrogance really began to swell. In my first two years of teaching, my cocky, unfounded self-belief helped me to develop practices that I thought were founded on logic and wisdom when in reality they were only based on what was best for me. What I began with the best of intentions, to help students, quickly morphed into what was best for my personal agenda. My reputation as a teacher quickly shifted from being seen as innovative and fun to being seen as strict and unbending. I didn't debate ideas, but simply believed that my way was the way. After all, my way worked when I was in school, when I was in college, and even at the very beginning of my career, so I believed it would continue to work every year after. If it didn't, the fault wasn't mine. The blame had to go to the kids, their parents, the community, the ineffective teachers who taught around me, and any other scapegoat I could manufacture.

You would think that after the sixteen rejections I faced chasing my first official leadership position just a couple of years into the profession I would have realized I didn't know it all. A sane, reflective, mature individual would have reflected on those experiences and questioned himself and what he needed to improve upon. Not me. I knew it all. The schools I had interviewed with were just missing out and had no idea what they had passed on. The fault was theirs, not mine, or at least that's what I told myself.

Far too often in schools we think our job is to have the answers. We think we are supposed to be the know-it-alls. In our classrooms, we teach from bell to bell without ever taking a break to breathe, let alone to hear from our students. At parent-teacher conferences we spend 15 minutes telling parents all that is wrong with their own child and what they need to do to fix it. We fight new fads, new research, new leaders, and anybody who does anything differently than we do. We think our way is the best way simply because it worked for us when we were children, or worse yet, because it's better for us as teachers today.

The truth is, over the last nineteen years, I have learned that teaching, effective teaching and effective leading, is about being a servant that is constantly on the hunt for how to support others. Because we are on the hunt to serve, we do not know it all. Our job is to make others feel smarter. To make others feel stronger. Our job is to help others be the best they can be, not just what we want them to be. My job as a teacher was not to work towards my next professional step. My job was to do the best I could, where I was, instead of always trying to position myself to be perceived as someone I wasn't. I had to quit trying to work for the next job and just start focusing on being the best I could be at my job. To do that I had to work on making my students, as well as fellow teachers, leave me always feeling smarter, stronger, more confident, and more competent. What I had been doing for so long was worrying about making sure everyone else thought I was smart and strong. I was more worried about what others thought about me instead of helping them gain greater confidence in themselves that I often created battles that weren't worth fighting.

Now in my career I work every day to try and make sure my students feel and believe that they are smart, they are kind, and they are loved. As a matter of fact, every time I get the chance to speak to students, whether it's with a microphone, on a PA system, or in a classroom, those are literally the words I tell them. I write them on desks. I write them on whiteboards. I speak them constantly, because I want those words to live inside of the students I am given a responsibility to lead.

I attempt to find the needs of my peers so that I can offer support. I do all I can to serve and as a result I am now in my second decade as a school administrator, have spoken to more than 50,000 educators across the country, have written a book that has been bought and read in every state across America, and now get the chance to share this message with all of you. Because I have grown to realize that not every fight needs to be fought. I have been able to support others more freely and begin to focus in on the fights that do need to be won. I focus on the future of others and not on my own wants. I focus more on keeping my mouth shut and allowing each word I do say to matter.

Each community and each building has its own understanding of what is taboo and what is not. Your job is to stick around long enough to shrink that list, to allow others to begin to open up to changing what really matters and embracing the good work already being done. As people begin to trust you, begin to value your input, and begin to understand your heart, opportunities to discuss what has been hidden will present themselves. If on the other hand, you enter into your school on a mission to change, to question everything, because your past experiences vary from your current reality, soon enough you will find yourself on an island looking for a new place to sell your vision. What worked in your past does not necessarily equate to what is needed for your present. Chapter 2 of this book is entitled, "Are you preparing students for your past or their future?" The same question can be asked here for leaders as they examine their role in the lives of teachers and staff. A leader's past helped create who they are, but does not have to be replicated by each teacher. A true leader works to identify goals and then designs the strategies to get there, using the people currently there.

Decisions that are made in schools often impact each group of stakeholders differently, staff, teachers, administrators, students, etc.... Just like with triangle decision making, the job of a leader is to facilitate productive conversations. When making a large level change, it is critical to identify which stakeholder groups should be addressed first, and quite honestly, I often look to win the support of those impacted the least, first. I know this sounds counter intuitive. Why would I work to win over individuals who have the least to gain? Big change often brings with it big emotions. Remembering the premise to assume the good and doubt the bad, we have to enter into change knowing that the status quo exists because good people did what they thought was best. Attempting to dislodge past practice can sometimes be perceived as a passive attempt to judge and indict intentions, whether or not that is reality. When emotions are involved, sometimes we as humans fall into the trap of arguing with people and not ideas. As an idea is just beginning to take shape, having a discussion with those who may not have a strong emotional connection and investment to the conversation may allow you the opportunity to refine your thinking while also recruiting supporters who are willing to discuss possibilities instead of debating realities. Like a snowball rolling downhill, the change initiative is no longer being carried by a lone snowflake. By the time it gets to those impacted the most, it is carrying the collective weight of all others who have bought in.

When I bit off the challenge to embrace a Standards Based Grading approach in one of my schools, I first got students to buy in. Having their support, allowed for easier conversations with parents who had their children championing for retakes, redo's, and less punitive grading policies. With parents and students on board, getting teachers on board and supporting their efforts became that much easier.

As an athletic director when I changed an athletic calendar to have boys' and girls' basketball held during the same season, I first approached parents to get their feedback, then I approached the coaches, and then finally the students.

No matter what the issue is, the goal is to not just to win support and supporters. The goal is also to elicit as much feedback as possible along the way. There have been times when I have received feedback from early groups that told me to abandon my ideas, feedback I should have listened to, but instead, out of my own stubborn drive, I plowed headlong into a minefield, or as stated earlier, a MINDfield. Instead of heeding advice from those without the emotional investment, I charged on, without support from others and without a refined argument, only to be left standing alone and without a cause to fight for in the end.

Do not create a list of strategies, a wish list of past professionals you want to work with again, and then spend all of your time measuring your progress in making your present look like your past. Look to the future and help guide others to get there. Whether you use your own Honolulu Blue or not is up to you. The takeaway is to focus on the people you have, earning their trust, supporting their dreams, and building brick upon brick, a foundation that will allow for a destruction of the taboo, not a destruction of reality or a rebuilding. The best leaders are those in the remodeling business, not the new construction business. Make sure you have solid floors and walls. Don't enter into anything new swinging a sledgehammer or you might just knock down a load bearing wall and the only one who will end up getting hurt is you. Be an architect for change. My blue binder is my blueprint. Do you have one?

 "If you want to change directions, you have to get going. Steering requires moving."

It's More Than a Title
Dr. Eric Carlin

Elementary School AP, Missouri, @Eric_Carlin

I had done it! I was officially an Assistant Principal and I had a name tag to prove it. I was off to a great start...so I thought.

This was one of my first observations that I was going to do on my own. After shadowing my principal, Dr. Rena Hawkins, the first month of school I was ready to go out on my own. I was holding tight to my rubric that was fresh on my mind from training and had high expectations of what I would see. As the observation began, I looked around the room and I felt like students were disengaged. The level of rigor and accountability seemed to be lacking. I placed my scores on the form and left the room. Later in the day, the teacher was speaking to Rena and became upset seemingly out of nowhere. Upon further discussion, the teacher opened up to Rena and said that she was upset with the scores that I had given her and felt that they were off point. Rena encouraged me to have a conversation with her sooner than later. I walked nervously to her room, deflated and not knowing what to expect from the conversation that was about to occur. We met and talked through the scores, the observation process, my thinking around the scores and hers. Leaving the room, I knew that I was confident in my observations, but I had missed something. After further reflection on that observation, I realized that I was missing one of the most important parts of leadership, trust.

When we step into the role of leadership we have to remember that we are people first and professionals second. A teacher's classroom is a daily representation of all of their years of schooling and countless hoop jumping, hours spent preparing their classroom, their raw passion for teaching and dreams of making a difference. In order to enter this space, that heart filled atmosphere, we first need to build trust. We have to start by getting to know teachers by getting out of our office and being present each day.

During the summer, when teachers are setting up their rooms, I use my size to my advantage and offer to help hang things on the wall or move large items around the room. When creating staff biographies of each teacher, I read their responses and play their favorite song on YouTube to get to know them a little better. As the year starts, Rena and I lead by example by putting ourselves out there and showing teachers (and anyone who watches) that we don't take ourselves too seriously. We have been seen making a "How to open a dumpster" video to ease teachers' worries about purging years of classroom materials as we re-configure buildings. Holding a guitar and singing our hearts out in front of a group of construction workers for a lip sync challenge. To creating an epic staff talent show where we can come together as a staff over breakfast, sharing laughs and making memories.

These things may seem like they have nothing to do with instructional feedback, but they have everything to do with instructional feedback. Trust with teachers starts by putting yourself out there and building relationships. When these relationships are formed, we can then start providing feedback that will have an impact.

Through hard work and intentionality, I have grown a lot over the past couple of years in administration and have built strong relationships with staff members, including the teacher from my first observation. I have become more aware during my observations and interactions with others that we are people first and professionals second. We have to earn trust before our feedback can become relevant!

BOLD NEXT STEPS

1. Identify the next initiative you hope to enhance or change. Do you know which stakeholder group: parents, students, staff will be most receptive and which will be most resistant? Which will you try to get on board first?

2. Can you create your own Web of Influence? Who influences your own decisions? Who do you influence?

3. List the three big projects that will define your next five years. Do you know the steps required to find success? Do you know what success looks like?

BOLD REFLECTIONS

CHAPTER SEVEN

DRILL AND KILL
DOESN'T WORK FOR
KIDS...OR ADULTS

I WAS A LUCKY KID. I grew up in a household that valued education. My parents wanted me to be a child, paving the way for me to later succeed as an adult. They constantly encouraged me to try new things. I was a Boy Scout. I played basketball, tennis, volleyball, football, baseball, and ran track. I was Student Council president, worked multiple part-time jobs, lived as a military brat attending 16 schools in my K-12 years, and always felt loved. I had so many varied experiences, diverse opportunities, in a wide array of settings, that each contributed to where and who I am today. Today I am a school administrator, a former teacher, a father of four, and an advocate for challenging and changing the status quo. Throughout my past, I was able to endure and often succeed, not because of the formalized schooling and learning opportunities afforded to me, but often, in spite of them.

Don't get me wrong. I had some amazing teachers, some people who were inspirational, compassionate, and kind, but I also had some teachers that were less than effective, not so courteous, not so gracious, and far from kind. I can remember the names of a few of the greats but have forgotten many of the others. School for me was less about my class and more about my teachers and my experiences. I know that is not the case for everyone, but for a child who moved around a lot, it was for me.

What We Do, They Do

As I look back on my childhood, I know I have modeled some of my career practices and some of my habits as an adult after those who set me on this path, even if subconsciously. I currently have a Doctorate degree, have attended law school, and continue to work towards other advanced degrees. I know a lot of this is attributed to the foundation that was laid by the schools and systems who worked to educate me and instill a passion for learning, but I am also a firm believer that the experiences I encountered, the people I met and the life I lived, has taught me far more than any worksheet, textbook, or assignment ever did. I can't tell you the titles of any textbooks I used in any class. I can't tell you what standards I mastered. But I can tell you about some of the amazing teachers, mentors, and peers who helped shape me into the person I am today.

I know I had some amazing influencers, some awesome teachers who allowed me to grow, fail, and learn. I had teachers who taught me by making learning relevant and relatable. I had teachers who sat down next to me and taught me on my level and used their influence to captivate me with experiences, not with lessons. They used their stories, their passion, and their genuine trust in me, to push me and grow me. It wasn't the lessons I learned in school that set me up for success. It was the people.

When I had my own classroom, I was an OK teacher. When I got my own school, I was a decent principal, but I am an awesome dad. I love being with my kids, both collectively and individually. Nothing brings me more joy than pulling into my driveway in the evening and having my kids all come running outside, eager to greet me. They know I have been at work all day and they know the power their hugs have to turn my day around. They know that just their presence makes me smile. Their simple gestures of affection are so powerful that they can alter my mood, my evening, and over time, can impact my entire outlook on life.

As their dad, my kids know how much I love spending time with them. Once a month I try to make it a point to take each of them out on a one on one date. I have stated many times in schools, "If you want to make a difference with every child, you have to make a difference with each child. Knowing the difference between EACH and EVERY is the difference." The same is true at home. It is important for me to impact all of my kids and one of the key ways for me to do so is to focus on each of them.

I see so much value in our simple one on one father-child dates. We have gone to the beach, to dinner, for ice cream, to Walmart, or even just for a walk. We don't do anything huge, but the accumulation of little things will have a huge impact. With each date, I get the opportunity to talk, share, and listen. Most of the time we are active and enjoying each other's company doing something fun, but I use these experiences to also try and share moments of wisdom. When driving with my youngest, I may make reference to why I allowed another driver the opportunity to pull in front of me in a parking lot and why it is important to take turns and share. With my oldest child, I may allow him to calculate tax and determine the right amount to tip on a bill. I may talk to my daughter about the shapes of the clouds or the planets we can see at night when looking out of my car's windows. I try to find ways to teach my children through the natural moments we have together.

When we return home though, my kids don't tell their siblings about teachable moments. They share the experiences. They share where we went and what we did. What they learned was taught with a subtlety that allows it to be embraced. The experience is what is remembered and what allows for a desire for repeated opportunities to learn.

My last book *It's Like Riding a Bike* (another shameless plug) embraces the statement "Once you learn how to ride a bike, you never forget" to help other educators learn the process for teaching students the skills that will last for a lifetime. The overarching theme throughout is that children do not learn enduring knowledge by sitting at a desk, but instead from getting outside and doing. Experience is the greatest teacher there is. Take a look at collective bargaining agreements in place between school districts and teachers' unions around the country to get a sense of this. It is the belief that experience matters that warrants the argument that financial incentives should be provided for teachers based on their years on the job. More years, more experience, more knowledge, more skill, more pay. Professional sports leagues respect this as well. Tremendous revenue is tied up in collegiate athletics, yet, we are learning that just because an athlete finds tremendous success at the college or high school level does not mean there is a guarantee for success at the professional level. There are rookie pay scales and veterans' exemptions allowing for athletes with more years of service to be compensated more. There is not always a guarantee of future success because of prior training. Sometimes teams are able to find a diamond in the rough by finding a player who may not have been a standout early on, but through a variety of experiences may end up becoming the GOAT (think the Tom Brady, quarterback for the New England Patriots - Greatest Of All Time---yes my Michigan bias is real).

College and Career Readiness

Our job in schools is not to equip students with the knowledge necessary for career success. Our job is to create students who have the skills necessary to keep learning, growing, and improving. We need to focus less on producing finished products and create students with the ability to keep gaining experience. With a renewed focus in America on creating students with College and Career Readiness, as so many of the standards describe them, let us remember, the focus is not knowledge, but skills. If you can ask Siri or Alexa for the answer to a question, you don't need to memorize it.

The same is true, not just for students, but teachers as well. Just as one of my titles is "father", I am also a "husband". I cannot spend all of my time just catering to my kids. My wife deserves individual attention as well. It can't always just be about the kids.

As a former principal at an inner city, high poverty school I had the unique opportunity to hire new teachers often. Working in a school like mine, and working with a principal like me, takes a toll on a teacher. I know I am not alone in this struggle. I have spoken to a number of other administrators who work in buildings very similar to mine. We discuss our need to find quality teachers to put in front of our amazing kiddos. In many districts, in many states, because of accountability measures, schools like mine, a school with a 90% poverty rating, a school with 30% of children having at least one parent in jail, and the struggle each year to achieve state academic achievement benchmarks to avoid intrusive mandates that could be imposed by legislators attempting to improve schools by cracking their accountability whips, there is a high staff turnover. As a result, so many schools with frequent openings, have very difficult decisions to make as we hire our teachers.

We know becoming a highly effective teacher is something that requires time and experience. So many of us understand that our first few years on the job were filled with missteps, struggles, and failures. We learned from our mistakes and got better and better with each successive year, yet we are faced now with a system that doesn't allow this growth to happen. Teachers are expected to step out of college, into classrooms of their own, and have everything figured out. These young teachers learn early on not to present vulnerability because this will be seen as incompetence. They will be evaluated out and will be asked to leave their schools within a few short years, before they ever have a chance to grow or become the masters they could develop into.

In athletics, players are allowed to red-shirt to gain knowledge and experience as they transition from high school to college and are allowed to learn from veteran older statesmen in their rookie professional years allowing them the chance to develop in the future. Lawyers are allowed to practice law for years before taking on their own firm. Doctors are provided multiple rotations and opportunities to practice medicine before being set free in their own office. Perhaps instead of expecting teachers to have all of the answers and all of the skills without the ability to gain experience we can begin to treat teachers with the same level of professionalism we give to people in other careers, with the true ability to be lifelong learners like we profess to value so much for our students. We need to allow teachers the ability to learn, grow, fail, and make mistakes early on.

What makes the first few years of teaching so valuable? Why does experience matter? Quite simply, the purpose of practicing is to improve. When we allow for the opportunity to practice, to reflect on progress, to improve, we learn. We cannot place teachers in a compliance driven environment, an environment where we ask them to simply follow the decisions of their bosses and expect that they will improve. This approach requires no reflection. No personal improvement. It is all about following rules, not about making new rules. It is in the formation of new rules, the development of new strategies that innovation develops. We will never grow creative teachers if administrators are only worried about developing compliant teachers.

The current curriculum available for teachers in every state provides for a solid foundation of knowledge, but the mindsets and practices we can put into place are what allow for true experiential learning and thereby real lasting learning. Humility is needed for any of us grow as weaknesses need to be freely revealed. Boldness can be harnessed as expertise is created. Only when we realize that expertise is not given, it is developed, can we truly begin to create a culture of excellence, a culture that models lasting learning and experience development.

I am a leader who has been intrigued by the "no homework" movement that has caught on in recent years. People such as Matt Miller and Alice Keeler have used social media to publicly state many reasons why they believe assigning homework can be harmful to students. Most significantly to me, is the idea that most of the homework that is assigned to students is based on low level content regurgitation. Students are asked to memorize facts and figures that have little relevance to their own lives and in order to complete these memorization tasks students are expected to remove themselves from the real world they actually occupy and sit in a sterile room and study flashcards or read a textbook. On the other hand, some will say that when teachers assign homework they are not just doing it to help students learn content. They may say it is also done to allow students to learn time management and organization. I believe that the teacher who assigns homework to promote a strong work ethic should have a strong enough work ethic to find another way. Many, myself included, do not see homework as harmful, but asking students to miss out on social activities, organic play, and family time to master learning that will not last beyond the next test, just does not seem to make much sense. Perhaps a better way for students to learn time management and prioritization is to allow for rich learning experiences through clubs, sports, and social environments.

If you are a parent of a school aged child who has attempted to help with math homework lately, you have no doubt heard the phrase, "That's not how my teacher wants us to do it." I heard this exact statement just last week as one of my sons was working on multi-digit multiplication. He was struggling with one of the procedural algorithms his teacher taught him so I attempted to show him another way. Unfortunately, because he was never taught with conceptual understanding in mind, what I attempted to explain made no sense. He was only focused on the process and not why it worked. If we don't understand the concept, our learning has very little relevance.

At my school district, we use a Standards Based Grading approach. We work to provide feedback to students and parents that is rooted in student learning, not just task completion. The idea is that our grades should reflect defined learning objectives and not arbitrary goals. The concept is sound, yet we have hit a few snags along the way, and I recently stumbled upon one of the reasons ...ME. Last week as I was having a conversation with a teacher about the grades for one of her students when I realized that I had been guilty of the same thing I had been accusing my son's teacher of doing. I had created a compliance driven culture instead of one focused on true understanding.

During the conversation with my teacher, I asked her to provide clarity for why a specific child had earned the letter grade of a B in her class. At my school, we still use letter grades although we are standards based to try and limit the disruption in communication with parents who still expect schools to look like it did when they were in the system. The teacher described her method of calculating the child's grade, a process that I believe should be relatively simple, but for this teacher it sounded more like calculating the gravitational pull of the sun. She discussed mean, median, and mode. She discussed weights of assessments, analyzing formative and summative results, and score regressions. She even threw the term "standard error" into the conversation even though she didn't really know what it meant. Seeing the puzzled look on my face as she was talking, she finally just said, "I thought that's what you wanted. I just wanted to do it right." Wow. This was a powerful moment for me.

I am a guy who writes books and presents in front of thousands of educators arguing that we need to focus on the product not the process. I tell leaders everywhere that compliance limits competence and in my own district I was creating a compliant teacher who just wanted to please me in an effort to do what was right. Some may say it's not a big deal. Some may say I am very lucky to have a staff wanting so desperately to make me happy and "do the right thing." I look at this and reflectively say that I have some work to do. The right thing should never be boiled down to what makes the leader happy.

As the leader, my job is to make sure every teacher is more comfortable answering "why" than they are "how". Teachers can spend their careers figuring out how. Figuring out why should be the destination that drives them. Needless to say, this conversation opened the door to some much needed coaching, both for the teacher and myself.

The recurring theme throughout this book is, teachers do what their leaders model. I am confident that many teachers assign homework simply because they feel like it is the expectation. Their principal sends e-mails at 5pm from his personal cell phone to his staff, interrupting countless family dinners, asking for responses before the evening comes to a close. Teachers are asked to chart student data, asked to evaluate assessment results, and lesson plan every evening. Teachers are given countless homework assignments of their own to complete so why wouldn't they assign homework to those they are charged to educate. Analyzing data, creating assessments, and lesson planning are all essential elements of the job. It would be difficult to argue that a teacher could be successful without incorporating these elements. Asking teachers to perform essential job functions while not on the job, however, that's where the problem begins.

Choice in Learning is Vital for Kids...and Adults

As a self-described lifelong learner, I like to spend my evenings reading, exploring Twitter, or chatting with other engaging educators on apps like Voxer. I take great pride in learning and do so regularly, exploring topics of interest to me, with people who are intriguing to me. We ask our students to explore the world around them. We want them to collaborate and utilize peers to grow. We ask our teachers to provide our students with opportunities to learn lasting skills, yet we ask teachers to perform socially isolating tasks, sacrificing their social and family lives, in an effort to improve. We tell them what data to analyze, what conclusions to draw, and what strategies to implement as a result. Instead, we need to provide our teachers with opportunities and strategies to reflect, to learn from others, to maximize the impact of experience, and limit the burnout that often has very little to do with instructing and facilitating students and a lot more to do with navigating through all of the hoops we make them jump through in an attempt to do things our way.

A key tenant of Bold Humility is creating confidence to grow competence. For far too long, we have focused more on compliance, at every level of our schools. I spend my time learning what I want, how I want, because I love to learn. When I am told not only what to learn but how, my motivation takes a nosedive.

If we want our students to become reflective learners, if we want to create a generation of individuals willing to grow through experiential encounters, if we truly value the art of teaching, we need to be sure teachers are treated as professionals and allowed the opportunity to explore their strengths, minimize their weaknesses and grow. The growth of our students depends on it.

I spent my first fifteen years in education as a teacher and administrator in Michigan. My parents made their home in Florida. This 1,000 mile separation encouraged me to make seventeen hour road trips multiple times a year so that my kids could spend time with their grandparents. As a father of four kids, I have been forced to make the transition to driving a minivan. It is not the sporty convertible I dreamed of driving when I was a teenager. My current ride is sprinkled with fruit snacks and animal crackers. It has a stroller tucked in the back and a cartoon inserted in the DVD player. I call my van my mobile classroom. My children are my students and I see every trip as a learning opportunity. With every trip, we have a destination in mind. We have a predetermined ending location, but it is often time within my mobile classroom that provides the greatest learning potential.

The first few times I made a road trip to Florida with kids in tow I decided to leave in the evening, to drive through the night, take minimal rest stops and just hurry up and get there. I believed the vacations didn't begin until I pulled into my parents' driveway. As a result, I often arrived exhausted, stressed out and ready to just hide until I recovered. Meanwhile, my kids were often fresh and ready to have the time of their lives. Because of this approach, I often dreaded vacations even though I really should have been excited about the prospect of getting away for a little while. For me, I was so focused on just surviving the drive that the drive was all I paid attention to. For my kids, often, they didn't remember ever being in the van. They were sleeping, watching movies, or locked in on some electronic device. Some would say this is a good thing, but the reality of them not even remembering 34 hours (17 hrs each way) of their vacation time, was a little concerning. It wasn't until my oldest child was five that I developed a new mindset.

We now leave for our road trips early in the morning. I want my kids to be wide awake as we drive so that they can embrace that the drive is a part of the vacation. Vacation does not begin when we get somewhere. It begins as soon as we leave. Think about this in terms of the students in your school. Our students are living their lives now. Their lives do not begin once they graduate. They are happening now. We can't let them just stay busy for thirteen years waiting for their real lives to begin. It is our job as educators to make sure that we are not simply preparing our students for a life in the future, but allowing them to live their lives today.

I want my teachers to embrace organic learning. I want them to equip students with skills that are transferable outside of their classrooms now and in the future. As I drive with my children in my mobile classroom I take full advantage of my captive audience to provide life lessons and content based learning. We discuss the changing geography of the landscape. We study cloud formations and weather patterns. We chart mileage and debate when and where to make our pitstops. We learn constantly through relevant and current experiences. This is how learning will happen for them in the future. It is how learning should happen now.

In the future, as adults, my own children will not be asked to sit behind a desk and complete a worksheet to learn how to solve a problem. They will not be asked to memorize algorithms and formulas. They will be asked to find and consult with experts. They will be asked to collaborate and share. They will be asked to analyze the world and synthesize information. They will be asked to reflect on their decisions and to improve their abilities. Again, if we want our students to behave this way, we must allow and encourage our teachers to teach this way.

We need to remind teachers that end of year assessments are important. They are A destination, not THE destination, and how we get there is up to them. Sure, we can just plow straight ahead, following a pacing guide and scripted curriculum and treat every day like its sole purpose is to get us closer to test day. We can spend an entire year so focused on a destination that our students lose sight of the fact that they are on a journey. We can make every school improvement goal focused on test data to reinforce our singular purpose and mission, or we can embrace a different mindset.

We can embrace the fact that our students and our teachers are on their journey right now. Everyday has its own opportunities and we can make each moment matter as much as the next. The destination is important, but not any more important than the day we are living in today. We need our teachers to have the freedom to follow detours, to take drives down country roads, to take a scenic highway, and whatever other adjustments are necessary and available.

There are multiple routes to take to go from Michigan to Florida. There are direct routes, scenic routes, routes that allow me to see new cities and towns, routes that may take longer than others. In schools, we tend to force teachers to follow one road, the road we traveled on or the road that will get us to our destination in the most direct way possible. Perhaps though, if we allowed teachers to take advantage of their opportunity to lead the drive each day, and this freedom allowed for detours to make the drive memorable, maybe, just maybe, teachers would be more inclined to make an 8 hr drive in their, "not so mobile," classroom every day an experience and not a chore and kids would be more inclined to stay awake and enjoy the ride. Maybe then we would get to our destination without the exhaustion and disheartened attitude that often greets us and the end of every day, week, and school year. We have to allow teachers the boldness to make the drive their own and provide them the resources to reflect along the way. Learning that lasts, whether for kids or adults, really requires three things. We must make it safe enough to fail. We must be strong enough to try again. And we must enjoy it enough to keep going.

 "Highly effective teaching is all about learning to REFLECT."

EMPOWERMENT IS MY SUPERPOWER
LAURA COKER

Instructional Coach, Florida, @LauraCoker09

Empowering students to become cognizant, confident thinkers and problem-solvers is one of the greatest gifts we can give our children. Excellent educators work to craft the skill and strategy of empowerment within the confines of their classroom. However, rarely do we as educational instructors identify the strategy of empowerment when describing the cultural community between administrator and teacher. I would argue that equipping teachers with empowerment over their instructional reasoning and understanding, as well as problem-solving of situations pertaining to students is a foundational pillar to student success in the classroom.

Teachers are taught early on in our careers that the best teachers reflect on their instruction and student learning to make adjustments and meet students' needs, but in all of my schooling, no one actually taught me how to reflect. No one ever explained to me the level of empowerment, handed over on a silver platter when authentic reflection transpires for teachers. Quality administrators inspire their teachers to think beyond what's directly in front of them and reflect on the bigger picture of their educational world. Thesis actions propels them to empowerment.

In the time that I worked with Dave, I watched him time and time again work to equip teachers with the skill of reflection. The ultimate reflection question was "How do you know that a day has been a good day or a bad day?" The answer to this question is not cut and dry and required all of us as educators to genuinely reflect on every facet of the day and how those components converge to construct the 'good' or 'bad' day. This empowerment through reflection extended to all areas. I would come to Dave with a problem or dilemma and I knew walking in that I was not coming to be given the answer. I was going to talk with him to show him my thinking and have him suggest a different perspective or angle in which to think about my problem. I always walked out of his office empowered to solve the problem myself. I was successful not because he told me the answers to my problems but rather because he empowered me to solve them myself. What a gift! I have now been outfitted with a way of thinking and reflecting that goes far beyond Dave being the administrator that I serve under. I can now multiply with others this skill of authentic empowerment through reflection.

BOLD NEXT STEPS

1. Examine your school's homework practices for both students and staff. Are there ways to limit what HAS to be done outside of school so that what CAN be done is accomplished?

2. Are there arbitrary deadlines that have been put in place in your class or school? Are you expecting tasks to be completed and learning to be mastered by predetermined dates? How can you eliminate or limit this practice by allowing all people to grow without fear of failure?

3. Examine ways for teachers or peers to seek advice and demonstrate vulnerability without punishment or consequence. Can people seek support anonymously or through designated support channels in non-evaluative ways that encourage and model growth.

BOLD REFLECTIONS

CHAPTER EIGHT

FEED ME

BEING A CHILD OF THE 1980S, I grew up on Chevy Chase, Steve Martin, and Rick Moranis. These guys were kings of nonsense and hilarity. To this day, if I see *The Jerk* or *Christmas Vacation* on TV, I will stop flipping channels and watch while I laugh hysterically. In 1986, one of the best "bad" movies ever came out. It was titled *Little Shop of Horrors*. Some of you may remember this movie. Rick Moranis stars as a flower shop owner who has the opportunity to display a Venus flytrap that feeds on humans, and notoriously begs the main character to "Feed me, Seymour." I guarantee the generation of kids growing up today would not find the same entertainment value from this movie that I did, but one thing remains constant. Just like the oversized plant in that movie, kids these days are screaming for us to feed them. They not only want the latest flavor of Doritos in their lunchbox, they also want us to feed their egos and self-esteem. And, yes, before you say otherwise, that is part of our job.

Kids will always live up to our expectations when they know what they are. All people will always rise to the level of the label they are given. Call a child an "A student" and you are likely to see him more willing to raise his hand and participate in class than the student labeled a "Struggling" or "Failing student". Call a child "at-risk", call him "gifted", call him a "disruption" and guess what you will get. It is up to us to redefine the labels kids are given and help them form identities of hope.

Ask a kid at your school today who Muhammad Ali was and most will be able to tell you he was a famous boxer. Ask who Cassius Clay was (hint, it's the same person) most won't have a clue. Athletes, rappers, and performing artists realize that creating a new persona and a new label for themselves helps to create a new identity. Katy Perry, Chad Ochocinco, Madonna, Eminem, have all created their own label for who they want you to perceive them as. Even I have worked to create a label I thought would be appealing to you. I did this when I chose the title for this book. Labels are not always bad. Bad labels are bad. On the flip side, some labels can instill hope and belief. I know when I graduated with my last degree and heard the announcement of DOCTOR Schmittou for the first time, I thought I was going to light the world on fire. Our students and our peers all deserve a stage name worthy of their potential, too.

Our Labels Can Define Student Success

As a child I loved the game of basketball. I still do. As an elementary school kid, I would stay up late watching my favorite athletes, The Detroit Pistons and The University of Michigan's Fab Five, and dream of one day wearing the same jerseys as my idols. Going into fifth grade I was a lanky 5'7", towering over my classmates. I was always the first one chosen to be on a pick-up basketball game with my friends and was frequently told I was "the best" player around and I believed it.

Fast forward to my 8th grade year. Those three years of middle school make a big difference for some boys. By the time I entered 8th grade, three years later, I was 5' 8". I had grown an inch since the end of elementary school. However, most of the other boys had grown a whole lot more. I was no longer the tallest. I was no longer the best. I was now the kid who was cut from his middle school basketball team and was told by his coach, I "was just not a basketball player." It was heartbreaking. I had spent the first twelve years of my life believing I could be great. Hearing others tell me I was good motivated me to practice daily and try to get better. It stoked my passion, but then, one opinion, from one adult, sent that all crashing down.

At the age of 13, I gave up because one adult made one value judgement about me. I know as a middle school coach, he did not have the time to develop me, to train me, to give me confidence, and fan the flames that were already burning inside of me. By the very nature of the "try out"/audition system, he was looking for the kids that already had the most talent. Unfortunately, his decision to cut me from the team killed my belief in myself. I know now that I would have never been a professional athlete, but I probably could have had a productive athletic career at least through high school if only given the chance. I wonder how often we have this same attitude within our classrooms.

We have pacing guides, time crunches, merit pay, and final exams. We look at our students and begin to make value judgements about who is already a refined student and who needs to be "cut" and dismissed. Because we can't just kick kids off of our roster, we give them a label, say they have special needs, blame their parents and community, send them to the office every day, and write them off without ever really coaching them up and helping them reach their potential. These students may not ever become professional writers, mathematicians, scientists, or teachers, but who knows what is burning inside of them.

This is not just a lesson for middle school educators though. Four years after giving up basketball, four years of choosing to work after school jobs instead of enduring tryouts and practice, I decided one evening to go to a local teen club we had in our neighborhood. At the time, I was living on the US Naval Base in Guantanamo Bay, Cuba and there wasn't much for high school kids to do. I was a Navy Brat so this club on base served as the local hangout for high school kids on the weekend. One Friday night in September I decided to stroll outside where the athletes and jocks normally congregated. On this particular Friday night, the varsity basketball team had organized their own pick-up basketball game. Still interested in the game, although no longer spending every waking moment practicing the game, I decided to stop and watch. As the game progressed, the trash talking among the players increased. The game was competitive, and the player's egos started to swell.

As the game ended, taunts and challenges were thrown out by the winning team as the losing team started asking for a rematch. The best player on the high school team was a kid named Allen. Allen was about six inches taller than me and looked like the amazing athlete that he was. Listening to the demands for a rematch from the losing team, Allen began walking away. As he walked off the floor, barking back at the players on the other side of the floor, Allen wasn't paying attention and crashed right into me as I stood there watching the scene. Having to protect his ego, he gathered his balance, got in my face and gave me a shove. In my head, all of the hooting and hollering that had just filled the air, immediately came to an end as all eyes were now on me. I'm sure the reality was not quite as dramatic, but I also know the crowd was fixated on what I was going to do. I'm not a fighter, but in that moment, I didn't want to back down either. I don't remember my exact words, but I replied with something equivalent to "You suck, Allen. You're not as amazing as you think you are." Lucky for me, Allen was not a fighter either. He started laughing, grabbed a basketball sitting on the sidelines, came back to look me in the eyes, and said, "Let's go. I'll show you how amazing I am." and he threw the ball at me.

The two of us then began to play a game of basketball, one on one, in front of the entire senior class. The game was a close one. Allen dunked on me a few times and I made a couple of three-point baskets to keep it close. With every basket I made, the crowd would erupt. Halfway through the game, with the crowd cheering at one of the baskets I made, Allen dug into his pockets and pulled out his car keys. He dangled them in his hands and announced to the crowd, "If this fool wins, he can have my car."

To make a long story short, I actually did win the game. Yes, it was a complete fluke. Allen spent most of the game trying to show off and made foolish mistakes. He had all of the pressure and I had none. But, I did win. As the game ended, and I was surrounded by my friends, Allen snuck out of the club, leaving his keys behind. I'm not sure how he got home that night, but I did NOT take his car. I had no need or desire for it because that night I regained something that had been lost four years earlier. I was asked by countless students why I was not on the team. I was told by peers that I had talent and I should have been pursuing it. Unfortunately for me, regaining my confidence, during my senior year, was too late for me to do anything life changing.

Looking back on it now, I often wonder how my life would have changed if I had continued to play basketball after eighth grade. Would I have made different friends? Would my confidence have transcended to other areas of my life? Would I have gone to a different college? I don't know, but what I do know is that as an adult today, I want to be someone who opens up opportunities and possibilities to kids. Who knows if I was a late bloomer, if I had one good game, or if my 8th grade coach just missed something when evaluating my talent, but I know this experience lives with me thirty years later. As teachers we need to inspire hope, not burst bubbles. That's why we got into this profession, or at least that's why I did.

My job is not to just teach kids content, but to teach kids how to dream. I want to fan the flames burning inside of every student, because once a fire is burning we can either feed it or smother it. Our students all have passions, hopes, and dreams. It is up to us to discover what they are, whether those dreams are athletic, academic, or social. Each child can be amazing at something. It is up to us to figure out what that something is so that they do not have to wait until years down the road to look back and remember when they used to love...before we as adults drove the love out of them. Be a dream builder for your students, your staff, and yourself.

Assume the Good and Doubt the Bad

When I was a principal, I attempted to model each day, optimism, hope, and celebrations of excellence. Many people from our generation still hear the word "principal" and think about a strict disciplinarian waiting to inflict punishments and consequences. Don't get me wrong. Principals do set the stage and determine the level of excellence expected, but this does not mean our job is to knock others down when they do not meet the expectations. Instead, we must view our role as one where we are reaching down to pull others up to where they can be.

In my school, we focus on affirmative grading. Instead of marking items wrong on assignments, teachers are asked to identify what students do correctly. Grades are all based on standards of excellence and not arbitrary, subjective leanings. I ask teachers to be cautious not to use their own bias to judge student success and, as such, I work diligently to maintain the same practice when evaluating teachers and other staff.

In most school districts across the country today, accountability is viewed as a swear word. I don't mean that we haven't always worked to own our successes and failures, but now, more than ever, teachers are working on the defensive. Annual contracts are the norm. Long gone are the days of tenure and immunity. As teachers begin to feel as though their jobs are on the line each time they are observed and evaluated, risk-taking and ingenuity are being driven out of the profession. Teachers find themselves stuck struggling to determine whether or not to appease the administrator who holds their career in their hand or the student whose destiny is in the balance. Unfortunately, these two worlds are not always in alignment. Just as students struggle with determining whether to conform or celebrate their diversity, teachers face the same struggles.

In my schools, I try to recognize that we are all growing and working to improve every day. I hope that the teachers in my buildings are better educators in May than they are in September. I hope that the feedback I am able to provide encourages growth and improvement. I believe that teachers are powerful people who have the ability to change destinies with their instruction and feedback. I believe that students need high quality people in their lives to become high quality people. I believe that students should not be penalized for what they don't know before receiving instruction, but that a teacher should determine deficits and work diligently to reduce weaknesses while also working to identify strengths. I carry the same burden as a leader when working with my staff.

I believe the purpose of staff observations and evaluations should never be to play "gotcha". We should never be looking to gather evidence of deficiency, but instead looking for evidence for improvement and of mastery. In my schools, I try my best to "grade" teachers as I expect teachers to "grade" students. In my last book, "It's Like Riding a

Bike:..." I detail what this looks like, but the premise is: mistakes happen, expect growth, grades should communicate progress, and we should never hold initial misunderstandings against anyone, if eventually understanding is acquired.

If I have done my job as a leader, I have hired individuals who are reflective and crave feedback. I have worked to become vulnerable and trustworthy. I have people in place, in strategic positions, who are able to help guide the progress of others and serve the needs of the school. As such, when I enter a classroom, leave feedback, whether it be glowing or growing in nature, it should be received and utilized for improvement. My job is not to knock down but to pull up. In Chapter 4, I discussed the use of Brag Tags and their ability to lift people and their practices up. What is celebrated is what is duplicated. For that matter, whatever is talked about, whether it be celebrated or discouraged, gets celebrated. This is why as a parent I get so frustrated when I find myself repeating myself over and over again. My good friend Brian Mendler says it best, "Become a second to last word teacher." If you harp on it, if you talk about it, it will be duplicated. We have to get comfortable focusing on excellence, ignoring (at least publicly) the struggling, and embrace the growth process.

We must recognize that we all have good days and bad days. We all have days where mistakes happen. We see this regularly in professional sports when our favorite athletes drop a pass, strike out, or crash before the finish line. We see this with authors who hire editors, actors who require multiple takes to film a scene, and recording artists who hire high priced producers to edit their vocal recordings. We cannot expect teachers to be perfect every minute of every day, just as we cannot expect students to cruise through the day without the occasional misstep. As an evaluator, I do not expect to walk into a classroom and see a well-rehearsed and choreographed play. I hope to see an organic, evolving learning space filled with risks, corrections, and improvements. My expectations are that I am able to provide a reflective lens where growth is fostered via the feedback I can provide. My job is not to always describe a better way of doing anything, but instead to identify areas of success or struggle that may have been overlooked and allow the teacher to develop a plan of action for further enhancement.

The obligation and responsibility is then on me to ensure that progress is made.

I do not believe in giving teachers mid-year "scores" or "ratings". I believe in giving teachers frequent updates and frequent goal adjustments. Just as I monitor my progress in running around the world (25,000 miles of running before I die) with a daily log, our teachers, much like Jules Verne, are trying to get around the world in 180 days. My job is to help them get there and to eliminate as many barriers to that success as possible. Just as teachers must own their own ability to grow EACH and EVERY child, as a leader I must own the same responsibility towards EACH and EVERY staff member. My success is dependent on their success. Their struggles are my struggles. I cannot sit back and own the data when it is positive and blame the teachers when it's lagging. I am in a fight with them and as such we all must work together. We often say people want to follow a leader with character, but in reality, we often follow leaders with clarity. Be sure others know who you are and what you stand for. This is what helps everyone move forward.

 "Knowing the difference between EACH and EVERY is THE difference."

WE ALL DESERVE MORE
ANONYMOUS TEACHER

Virginia

I was a new teacher five years ago at my school just outside of Virginia Beach, VA. I got into education because I wanted to change lives. I didn't sign up to teach because I wanted summers off or because I thought it would be easy. I signed up for this job because I thought it was my calling and I wanted to change the future. One year into my career, however, and I wanted out.

I didn't experience anything traumatic. I didn't have an angry parent conference or a hostile parent. I just felt like I didn't matter. I felt alone. I felt isolated. I felt like just another cog on the assembly line.

During my first few weeks on the job, I was told by my administrators that I was supported. I was told that they would have my back, but the truth is, they just never got around to modeling those words. I get it. Their jobs are busy. I honestly believe they wanted to support me and probably thought that leaving me alone would serve me best, but the truth is, their lack of feedback, conversation, and consultation made me feel like I just wasn't important to them.

I often hear about how teachers are leaving the profession in droves. I have heard people say it's because we don't get paid enough or the kids are just too hard. I don't believe that. I knew those would be factors before I signed up. The truth of the matter is that I almost walked away, not because the pressure was too intense, but because I just didn't believe in my power anymore. I thank God that in year two another new teacher was hired to work in my building. I thank God that she had the same idealistic visions of success that I started my career with. I thank God that the two of us are now best friends who lean on each other, push each other, inspire each other, and help keep it real. We all deserve to feel powerful. We all deserve the opportunity to grow. I am grateful that just as I was ready to walk away, I met someone who grabbed onto me and has not let go since.

BOLD NEXT STEPS

1. Find out what your students/staff really think about you. Create a survey or anonymous poll where opinions on your leadership and instructional practices can be critiqued, then share those results publicly. That vulnerability will also help hold you accountable for taking action.

2. Find out at what age your students/staff learned to tie their shoes, ride their bikes, or brush their teeth. Were you always "on pace" with the norm? What can you change about your practice that acknowledges that each person learns at a slightly different rate?

3. Reach out to another teacher and ask for help. Do not give them feedback; ask for it yourself. Be vulnerable. Be real. Be BOLD.

BOLD REFLECTIONS

CHAPTER NINE

WHO I AM TODAY

I HAVE BEEN an administrator for more than half of my career. There are some who would argue that I have lost touch and didn't teach long enough to really learn the craft. There are others who would argue that I am lucky to have had an early start on learning all of this leadership stuff. At this point in my career, I am confident enough to say both views are accurate. I wish I could have spent more time refining my pedagogical craft, but I am also so grateful that I have had so many years to make so many mistakes and improve who I am and what I do with each passing year.

I became a full-time administrator at the age of 30. I had the confidence to do the job, but made more mistakes than I care to admit. In my first year as an administrator, I even got a child who was completely innocent, grounded at home and suspended from school. It was my first month on the job in my new role and I was doing all I could to be the supportive leader I was hired to be. I wanted the teachers to know I had their backs and students to know I had high expectations. I stood with my arms crossed in the middle of the hallway during passing time, each day, scowling at students while smiling sweetly to every teacher. By the beginning of October, I was beginning to believe I really had the job figured out. That all changed quickly.

As I was standing in the hallway one Friday afternoon I was approached by an upset and extremely agitated teacher, Mrs. S. Mrs. S. was guiding one of her seventh grade students, Brett, towards me by holding his elbow. She got within five feet of me and began to unload. According to her, Brett had just passed a note to a young girl in her class that would have fit neatly into a chapter of *Fifty Shades of Gray*. As she handed me the note and I started reading, I felt myself blushing as a result of the words I was reading. When I turned my gaze from the paper to the twelve year old boy standing in front of me, my embarrassment turned to rage. How dare this boy write something so vile and crude to such a sweet little girl? Twelve year olds had no business knowing some of the words this boy was writing. Telling Mrs. S. I would take care of it, I escorted Brett to my office so that I could pass out some justice.

After giving Brett a strong lecture, I went to my computer, looked up the name "Brett" in the student information database, called Brett's dad, and sent the young hoodlum to my secretary where he was to wait to be picked up before enjoying a few days out of school.

Friday came to an end. I went home for the weekend proud of my ability to teach responsibility to a twelve year old boy, the star of the middle school football team, and help teach respect for girls at the same time. Two days later I returned to work still feeling triumphant and celebrating my ability to do my job so well. As I approached my office I was stopped by my secretary. Before even receiving a "Good morning", I was told, "We need to talk". She stood up, followed me into my office, turned on my light, and started talking while I set down my bag. She told me I had messed up, royally. Apparently at my school, there were three seventh grade boys named Brett. The boy who wrote the note was named Brett M. The boy whose father I had called was Brett C. When I had gone to my computer on Friday to look up Brett's contact information, I had just typed in his first name and assumed the first name that came up was his. As a result of my mistake I had let a guilty student go free, had condemned an innocent child to a weekend of disastrous proportions, and now evidently had the father of the innocent child waiting to see me to discuss the fact that his child was still swearing on his life that he didn't do it.

Before confronting the father waiting for me in the lobby and explaining my error, I instead picked up my office phone and called my principal. I explained to her what I did and began to apologize repeatedly. She cut me off, telling me that she would be right there and would help fix it. She was a master. In front of the father, Brett (the innocent), and me, my principal went on to explain that everyone makes mistakes. She could have scolded me. She could have thrown me under the bus, but instead, she used this as a teachable moment for us all. She took a moment that could have and probably should have been handled very differently and instead decided to extend grace. Grace taught me more than any lecture or punishment ever could have. She knew that mistakes have the power to teach and as her assistant, her role was to teach me and help me improve. She knew I was not a finished, polished product. She knew that ignorance can be corrected when taught and teach she did. She did for me what I expect each teacher to do for each student. This doesn't mean I stopped making mistakes and perfected my craft, but it does mean she allowed me to learn and understood that learning is a process. Learning is not a proverbial lightbulb moment. Learning, lasting learning, often involves stumbles and missteps all along the way.

As I grew in my confidence as a young administrator, I am humbled to say, more doors opened for me and soon I was a principal in charge of my own school. I was a man charged with the task of not only helping students grow and learn, but doing all I could to place the most competent and capable adults in front of those same students. As a principal, that responsibility often led to some very difficult decision making. In the age in which we live and work, it saddens me to admit that there is a shortage of quality teachers available in the workforce. Due to a lot of the factors already mentioned, many of the world's brightest and best have been discouraged from joining the ranks of our noble profession making it that much more important to seek out, find, and retain amazing teachers wherever they can be found.

In professional and collegiate sports, the expectation is that coaches and managers spend days on the road scouting talent, looking for individuals who will improve their teams. In K-12 schools often when a teaching position opens up administrators will post their opening on a static job announcement board and then sit back and wait two weeks to see who applies and then sift through resumes of unknown individuals. Law firms, hospitals, athletic teams, and even the military know that in order to get the best talent, they must go find the talent. They send recruiters into schools, are active on social media, and market themselves all over a variety of media platforms to give themselves a sense of credibility and therefore desirability to prospective employees who are looking to become a part of something great. As an administrator, I know that my teachers have a bigger impact on students than curriculum, programs, resources, or me. I made a decision early in my administrative career that as the leader I would spend whatever time was necessary finding the best candidates possible. I wasn't looking for the most polished teachers. I was looking for those with the most power to grow and change lives.

March, April, and May are the busiest months of the year for me. Aside from state testing season, school and district improvement planning, scheduling, and my own kids' social calendars, this is also the time of year that I begin my recruiting efforts to find the best teachers possible for the following school year. In March I begin making social media posts describing my desire to hire life changers and destiny shapers in my school. In April I begin crisscrossing the country meeting with people who I have met at conferences and through social media or associates to convince them to join my team. In May I spend time at universities and college campuses to elevate our profession and work to convince new and future graduates to entertain teaching as a career of choice.

I am always recruiting whether I have vacancies or not. It's not because I am looking to move out the old and bring in the new, but my charge is to give each child the greatest opportunity for success. I may not always have a teaching vacancy, but I am yet to have a year go by with zero openings available the following year. Just like a young baseball player would be excited to be drafted to play for a minor league affiliate of the Yankees if it meant he had an opportunity to one day play in the big leagues while working on improving his skills today, the same mindset and strategy is used in my schools. Paraprofessionals, secretaries, and cafeteria workers are often certified teachers learning the craft, adapting to our culture, and enhancing kids' lives in whatever role they have while waiting for an opportunity to get their own classroom. Because of the value we have placed on being a part of the team, we are able to find people willing to work for less money just to be a part of our team.

I have been accused of always hiring young. The truth is I always hire for potential "over proficiency." My job is to teach teachers and help them grow and that means looking for individuals who may not be as polished as others, but with coaching and support have displayed evidence of a ceiling much higher than their peers. Experience does matter. A great resume is what will get an individual an interview. A personality displaying potential and humility will get an individual a job.

Just last year an individual sent me a message on social media saying, "Quit hiring such young moldable teachers and stick with what has always been successful." I am sure they meant this as an insult, but the truth is every word of this message makes me smile, because even in their presumed disagreement they were acknowledging that I was hiring individuals with the ability to adapt and change the status quo, people willing to do whatever was necessary, even if it meant doing things differently than had always been done.

As a principal, every Friday I spent my afternoons at the playgrounds in one of the three housing projects in which my students lived, pushing kids on swings, talking to parents, and spreading the love. I spent every morning, hugging students, telling jokes, and spreading optimism. I spent my evenings worrying, and filled with anxiety, hoping that all that I had given had been enough to change destinies. I know I cannot do it alone, none of us can, so I have to hire others willing to do it right alongside of me, people willing to inspire me when I feel like other things are more important. I hire people who are able to connect with those with whom I cannot.

We are all the products of those we work with. None of us are self-made. Knowing this, I work tirelessly to surround myself with others who make me better just as I own the responsibility to also enhance the lives of those who work with me. Because I know I don't know it all, I am on a constant quest to learn, grow, and steal from those who I admire. I am bold enough to say that everything I know I learned from someone else. We all know that the best teachers are professional thieves. They steal the ideas from others and then adapt them for their own use. I am no different. Most of what I do is a result of stealing ideas of some of my edu-heroes: Rick Wormeli, Quinn Rollins, Dave Burgess, Beth Houf, Adam Welcome, Rena Hawkins, Tara Martin, Brian Mendler, etc... The pipeline of stolen ideas flows freely from my heroes, through me, and into my teachers. Much of the success that the students in my schools have achieved has been a result of the amazing teachers who work tirelessly to inspire, create, and enhance the lives of everyone they encounter and I know that often my job is to simply play intermediary between those with the original thoughts and those who are charged to make the impact.

Today as I write this I am sitting outside, in Michigan, on a beautiful August night, blessed because of those who have allowed me to continue to enhance my influence. I began my career with a captive audience of 120 students each day in my own classroom. I moved on to lead individual schools and now get to work beside others at the district level. I am now the Executive Director of Curriculum and Instruction for a school district that is filled with life changers. I am one week into my new job and am already so excited by all that I see. We are a district with tremendous potential because we have tremendous heart, passion, and ambition. We have tradition and history, but more importantly, we have a desire to look to the future. We know we have children today who depend on us to help them create our tomorrow and I can't wait to see what we can do.

In this role, I get to work with building leaders as they serve as change agents and beacons of hope. I get to work with teachers who inspire and motivate while informing and shaping minds. Bold humility is on display in this district in a very real way and that is part of what intrigued me to make the move. My hope is that I am able to continue to work beside amazing influencers of hope and that those of you who are reading this will continue to inspire me with your ideas and inspiration. Tweet me, message me, and let me know what you are doing to bring about greatness. What you do today, might just impact my students tomorrow.

SERENDIPITOUS ENCOUNTERS
ALLYSON APSEY

Elementary Principal, Michigan, @allysonapsey

In my first year of teaching, I distinctly remember one very difficult day. Things in the classroom were spiraling out of control and I walked into the staff bathroom and stared at myself, wondering if I had made a mistake with my career choice. In that moment, I didn't turn to a colleague or a mentor because I was too embarrassed and felt alone in my struggles. I did not realize that all educators experience these same challenges at one time or another.

Some educators spend their entire careers isolated, which fuels self-doubt and loneliness. It doesn't have to be this way. When I moved to a new, larger district, my six elementary principal colleagues became a resource for ideas, a sounding board, and my friends. In addition, I became a connected educator through Twitter, which led to a professional learning network that spanned the country and the world. In addition, I have a school building full of creative and smart teachers and support staff. I will never again hole myself up in my office to try to figure out a plan. I first reach out to my colleagues and then my larger network and the ideas come pouring in.

In 2015, I began to share my journey and my reflections on a blog (allysonapsey.com) that lead to publishing a book called The Path to Serendipity, and my journey continues as I get set to publish my third book and travel the country as a national speaker. I am who I am today because of all the generous educators who share their own stories and encourage others to do the same. Now, it's your turn.

BOLD NEXT STEPS

1. Promote your school. Take some time tonight and identify the strengths of your school. As a leader, you may think you are paid to fix problems, but one of the best solutions to any problem begins with a positive outlook. Sell your greatness to those in your social circle, whether in person or online.

2. Identify the strengths of those who work with you. Your job is to elevate and inspire others to grow. Sit down, face to face, with those you depend on and tell them why they are so good.

3. Who inspires you? Find them, tell them, and thank them.

BOLD REFLECTIONS

CHAPTER TEN

TWEET
WORTHY SUMMARIES

INTRO: If we want to create kids who become high quality people, we must be adults of high quality.

Chapter 1 Don't ever begin a sentence with, "I can't wait until..." Embrace today and go all in.

Chapter 2 As educators, our job is not to create lessons, but to establish memories.

Chapter 3 The best teachers are extremely mature with childlike personalities.

Chapter 4 It is our job as educators to make sure that we are not simply preparing our students for a life in the future, but allowing them to live their lives today.

Chapter 5 The job of a principal has three components: hire the best, support the best, cheer on the best.

Chapter 6 Being a leader means we assume the good and doubt the bad.

Chapter 7 Knowing the difference between EACH and EVERY is the difference.

Chapter 8 Kids will always live up to our expectations when they know what they are.

Chapter 9 Your job is never to knock others down. It is always to reach below and pull others up.

Chapter 10

Follow me and some of my edu-heroes:

@daveschmittou
@rickwormeli2
@jedikermit
@burgessdave
@BethHouf
@mradamwelcome
@renathunderhawk
@taramartinEDU
@BrianMendler
@allysonapsey
@onesweetbatch
@Eric_Carlin
@LizRibaudo
@emiliyleach14
@LauraCoker09
@santiagoAM115
@jenquattrucci

MORE FROM EDUGLADIATORS

R.E.S.U.L.T.S.: Promoting Positive Behavior and Responsibility for Learning

by Krista Venza (@kristavenza) & Jon Treese (@jt2510)

R.E.S.U.L.T.S. is a book that provides applicable strategies for teaching students to make positive choices, take necessary action and promote growth. This book is an enjoyable mixture of inspiring stories and a framework that promotes positive behavior and responsibility for learning. From R.E.S.U.L.T.S., educators will feel empowered to make a difference in the lives of their students. Let this book encourage you to possibly rediscover the importance of building connections with students. Included in the book is an account from one of Jon and Krista's former students who has benefited from educators who have never given up on her. Her story is an inspiring account of what hard work, drive, and a resilient spirit looks like.

Champ For Kids
by Kelly Hoggard (@champforkids)

This book is for every teacher, no matter their level of experience. For seasoned veterans confidently navigating around the ring, find inspiration to continue to push on into the next round. For educators that feel as though every time they get on their feet, they are bruised and battered by another jab, make connections to this book to help develop a solid foundation towards becoming a champion. Finally to preservice educators standing outside the ring unsure if they have what it takes when the day comes to be tagged in, find the guidance and essentials needed to head into the ring. Champ For Kids inspires advocacy, going to the ropes for students, coaching them through mistakes so they land the TKO!

The Future Is Now: Looking Back to Move Ahead
By Rachelle Dene Poth (@Rdene915)

If we are dedicated to facilitating the best futures for our students, we must be fully invested in lifelong learning and our personal and professional growth. In this book, the reader will hear from different educators, each sharing anecdotes and wisdom about becoming more connected, taking risks, and using failures and past experiences to help prepare for the future. Inspirational quotes appear throughout, prompting introspection and a call to action. A student also lends her perspective in a chapter, offering reflection from the other side of the classroom. When we strengthen ourselves as educators, we in turn empower others to do the same. Stronger together, we face whatever the future of learning will bring.

ABOUT THE AUTHOR

Dr. David M. Schmittou is a father of four, a former classroom teacher and building principal, now living in Michigan where he serves as Director of Curriculum and Instruction. He has written several books, most recently, *It's Like Riding a Bike: How to Make Learning Last a Lifetime*. Dave has had the opportunity to speak at many national and state level conferences and can often be found working with local districts as they begin to examine standards-based grading, effective leadership, and creating strategies that embrace the process and the products of learning.

Feel free to contact him directly on Twitter @daveschmittou or follow him on Instagram @schmittou.

Manufactured by Amazon.ca
Bolton, ON

12955653R00085